CANADIAN FEMINISM
AND THE LAW

CANADIAN FEMINISM AND THE LAW

The Women's Legal Education and Action Fund and the Pursuit of Equality

by

SHERENE RAZACK

SECOND STORY Press

FEMINIST PUBLISHERS

CANADIAN CATALOGUING IN PUBLICATION DATA

Razack, Sherene

Canadian Feminism and the law

Includes bibliographical references and index.

ISBN 0-929005-19-8

1. Women's Legal Education and Action Fund – History.

2. Women – Legal status, laws, etc. – Canada.

3. Women's rights – Canada. 4. Feminism – Canada.

I. Title

KE4399.R39 1991   342.71'0878   C91-093462-2

KF4483.C57R39 1991

Printed and bound in Canada

Edited by Beth McAuley

Second Story Press gratefully acknowledges

the assistance of the Ontario Arts Council

and the Canada Council.

Published by

SECOND STORY PRESS

760 Bathurst St.

Toronto, Canada M5S 2R6

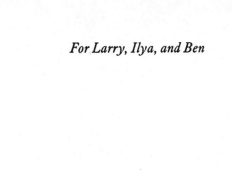

For Larry, Ilya, and Ben

CONTENTS

ACKNOWLEDGEMENTS

Books and theses are notorious for devouring friendships and family ties. In my case, even though I have treated many friends recklessly, I have had around me a steadfast and generous community of supporters. I owe a great debt of gratitude to my teachers at the Ontario Institute for Studies in Education for three and a half years of unfailing intellectual support. In particular, my advisor Ruth Roach Pierson inspired me with her commitment to feminist history, bolstered my flagging spirits, and never failed to come up with well-timed suggestions of sources to consult or ideas and opportunities to pursue. Dwight Boyd, Marjorie Cohen, Mary O'Brien, and Alison Prentice offered their intellectual guidance warmly and readily. The women of LEAF, the "subjects" of this work, made the research possible by agreeing to be interviewed, sharing files, and displaying through it all their remarkable adeptness in reflection. A number of people, too numerous to name, believed in this project before I did, got excited on my behalf, had brilliant ideas, consoled and encouraged me beyond measure. To my family, friends, and colleagues (I hope you know who you are), my heartfelt gratitude. I dedicate this work to Ilya and Ben, who taught me to step out of myself, and to Larry Brookwell without whose strength and commitment I could never have been free to write.

"Wrong Rights":
CHALLENGES OF APPLYING
FEMINISM TO LAW

IN HER ARTICLE entitled "Wrong Rights," Elizabeth Wolgast offers the following argument: "Rights work where people are in a position to press for them; for others they give only the caricature of justice."[1] Over the past ten years, in one way or another, the language of rights has been central to the work I have done for pay. I spent most of my time as a human-rights educator trying to dress the daily realities of oppression in the language of rights, aware that the exercise reduced that experience profoundly and believing that rights were something worth having. I worked from the premise that there could be no rights without means, as Wolgast clearly does in this quote. Social change was all about getting the means (power) to insist that one's rights claims be honoured. It did not occur to me then that my experience, and that of other women and minorities, might never be fully accommodated within the construct of rights. The unease I felt, but did not acknowledge, with rights thinking pushed me to search for the potential of the feminist project in law and at the same time to ask those questions that came from the spaces of my personal experience as a woman of colour, spaces in which I filed away difference and powerlessness.

To understand feminism applied to law and to gauge its potential to transform women's lives, I focused my exploration on a very specific historical project: the study of the Women's Legal Education and Action Fund. LEAF, a relatively new feminist organization founded in 1985, emerged from the historical context of Canadian women organizing in the early 1980s for constitutional guarantees of sex equality. It can be located, at first glance, within the sphere of what is often too glibly called mainstream feminist activities. Because of its relative youth, LEAF had, at the time I began this work in 1987, a fairly skimpy history. It had shepherded only a dozen or so cases through the legal system, and final decisions were pending on most. It did not take long, therefore, to peruse the legal documents pertaining to its cases and to come to the conclusion that these documents told a particular kind of story about the feminist project that is LEAF. They told a story of women stretching rights language to almost unrecognizable lengths in order to introduce into a court of law some of their realities as an oppressed group. As the story continued to unfold in the legal documents I examined, it illuminated the limitations of rights language and clarified how the particular knowledge systems, or the discourse of which rights language is a part, might be manipulated to express a more woman-centred view of the world.

Although I took the inquiry to the end of 1988, with occasional updates, the picture of LEAF that emerged was one of an organization at the beginning of its history. LEAF has continued to evolve, and its various projects, which constitute the feminist movement in Canadian law, have taken at the time of writing some interesting and positive new directions. The historical portrait of LEAF and the introductory overview of the theoretical challenges of applying feminism to law lay, what I hope to be, the basis for a discussion of what can be gained and lost from pursuing equality in law.

What's Wrong with Rights

Rights thinking permeates our everyday lives and shapes many feminist activities so deeply that it is often difficult to remain self-conscious of the limits it places on our seeing and knowing. As women, we often resist the construction of gender that comes out of rights language while simultaneously working with it to improve our daily lives. The notion of rights, and of equality, is inescapably bound to the notion of justice, for both feminists and non-feminists. It forms a part of our everyday understanding of right and wrong. When women and other oppressed groups articulate the problems of our daily lives using the concept of rights and all that it entails, we are consciously or unconsciously squeezing our lived experience into a pre-ordained mould. In tracing the contours and historical origins of this mould, we gain some insights into what rights language enables us to acknowledge and what it demands that we suppress.

Much of the basis for thinking about rights in law today comes to us from white male liberal theorists, who interpret and expand upon the great liberal thinkers of the nineteenth century. Liberalism, as one of its most well-known contemporary exponents John Rawls[2] developed it, is about justice, fairness, and individual rights. The bedrock on which these three concepts lie is the view that there must be no arbitrary distinctions between individuals because we are rational human beings, and because each individual has "his [sic] own aims, interests, and conceptions of the good."[3] The fundamental term of our association with each other is our respect for each individual's liberty to pursue his or her own interests; interests, however, that very often collide with the interests of others. Classic liberalism places considerable emphasis on the autonomy of individuals and their relationship to each other in this spirit of competition. Because competing claims must be resolved, my right to do as I please has to be circumscribed by principles of justice to which we all agree.

Three observations are in order concerning the concept of rights in liberalism. First, and most obvious, principles of justice are of the highest importance because they enable us to evaluate and rank competing claims. Second, our most distinguishing feature as individuals is our capacity to reason, that is, our capacity to identify and to work for our own interests. Third, liberalism is based on a fundamental separation between reason, and desire or emotion, with greater importance given to reason. Roberto Unger, well-known for his critique of liberalism, reminds us that this separation in liberal thought must be understood as an explanation of the nature of being, as a "metaphysical conception of the mind and society,"[4] and not just as a doctrine about the disposition of power and wealth.

Liberals hold these ideas in common regardless of how else they may differ, and from them they derive a number of related concepts such as equality, equal opportunity, and the concept of community.

Equality, for liberals, can mean the equal right to benefit from one's natural talents. However, most liberals have moved beyond the classic notion of meritocracy. They choose instead a notion where the inequalities created at birth are mitigated by social policies that have as their aim a redistribution of society's benefits. For instance, Ronald Dworkin has written of the two components that make up this concept of equality:

> The first is the right to *equal treatment*, which is the right to an equal distribution of some opportunity or resource or burden.... The second is the right to *treatment as an equal*, which is the right not to receive the same distribution of some burden or benefit, but to be treated with the same respect and concern as anyone else.[5]

The redistributive justice envisioned by Dworkin operates, in the liberal view, to counter disadvantages created by fate – an arbitrary distribution of natural and social contingencies. John Rawls also moves beyond the principle that an individual's freedom to pursue his or her own interests should be paramount. Rawls's ideal society would also accept what he calls the "difference principle," which adopts equality as a primary goal and which acknowledges that individuals who are unable to press their rights claims as a result of poverty or ignorance do, in fact, enjoy less liberty than others and must be compensated accordingly. Rawls is thus able to argue for going beyond the ideas of mere equality of opportunity and meritocracy to the concept of a society where the choice of what is needed by less privileged members of that society may dictate which individual's claims or rights we honour as just.[6]

Underlying liberalism, either in a Rawlsian version or in that of others, is a concept of a self who has an independent existence unconnected to other selves or defined by the ends it chooses. Individuals are free to choose what they like; the major constraint on their choice is the principle of respect for another's capacity to choose, and to Rawls and Dworkin's theories one can add considerations of redistributive justice. It becomes difficult to speak of group needs and interests, or to speak of the individual in his or her community given this premise of a decontextualized self.

Communities appear to have little relevance to individuals, and when liberals attempt to grapple with the notion of community, problems arise. For liberals such as Rawls, a community is made up of individuals who agree to the original principle of justice; but, the community seems to have a life of its own beyond the individuals in it when it begins to possess each individual's talents, and, more importantly, when it begins to regulate the way these talents operate to limit or enhance an individual's rights claim.

Not surprisingly, it is the liberal notion of self which most offends its critics. Michael Sandel has noted that Rawls's concept of self appears disempowered in spite of the autonomy and independence that it supposedly possesses. Pointing out that an individual is not independent but instead has all kinds of ties, emotional attachments, and a personal history, Sandel writes:

> To imagine a person incapable of constitutive attachments such as these is not to conceive an ideally free and rational agent, but to imagine a person wholly without character, without moral depth. [7]

Legal thinking is based upon the liberal notion of self, and thus it has inherited the abstraction and limits of this concept. Modern western law, of course, takes pride of place in the liberal scheme of things, its function being the adjustment of competing claims. [8] Those who criticize the law on the basis that it amounts to nothing beyond liberal legalism have relied on the same critique Michael Sandel makes about the nature of the liberal self. For instance, Naomi Scheman describes the law and the liberalism on which it is based as embodying "an anti-communitarian view of how society ought to work." [9] Humans are not seen as beings who are socially constituted, that is, "as having emotions, beliefs, abilities, and so on only in so far as they are embedded in a social web of interpretation that serves to give meaning to the bare data of inner experience and behaviour." [10] This is also what Robin West means when she asserts that "the human being assumed by legal theory precludes the woman described by feminism." [11]

In sum, the concept of an independent, decontextualized self functions to suppress our acknowledgement of the profound differences between individuals based on their situation within groups and the profound differences between groups. Without a theory of difference, we cannot make clear what the relationship is between groups or communities. Finally, what this notion most inhibits is our understanding of power as something other than the power of one individual to assert his or her claim over another's. It is difficult to explain oppression, that is, the consistent dominance of the claims of one group over another, with this one dimensional and individualized view of power. Further, it is a framework that effectively shuts out opportunities to propose new relationships not predicated on the concept of individuals in competition for pieces of the pie.

The Group Rights Approach

Those who reject the liberal self are immediately confronted with the question of where the self ends and community begins. If they remain within a rights framework, that is, accepting justice as fairness and thinking in terms of competing claims, the problem becomes complex indeed. To illustrate: A common response to the liberal concept of the independent self is to insist on putting back the context so easily removed in the liberal model. Thus, one can argue for the rights of women as a group, who possess a certain group situation (inequality) that requires a group remedy, by saying that who an individual woman *is* relates to the fact that she is a member of that group (women), a condition affecting her individual identity. [12] In effect, this approach suggests that no individual is ever really autonomous, and in evaluating rights claims we are obliged to consider the contexts in which individuals operate.

Kenneth Karst tries to contextualize the concept of self when he pleads for the replacement of the "ladder" view of rights, a hierarchical view of rights which ranks the claims of autonomous individuals according to abstract principles of justice, with the "web of connection" view of rights. Referring to Carol Gilligan's work on a morality based on an ethic of care, Karst would "feminize" rights by looking "beyond the idea of rights as personal zones of non-interference to a conception of justice that recognized our interdependence." [13] A rights approach based on an ethic of care, however, has to occupy a metaphysical universe: we still have to understand the nature of self and being. An ethic of care, as Joan Tronto points out, has to establish the boundaries of our caring and the relationship that ties various "webs" of caring together. In other words, it has to define community, and "there is nothing inherent in community that keeps it from being oppressive toward women and others."[14] When Karst and others speak of putting caring and connection back into the rights model, they do not take up these fundamental questions any more deeply than do traditional liberals.

The failure to define self and community exposes us to the risk of universalizing experience. For this risk means, in Alice Jardine's words, "simply translating 'woman as concept' from one culture to another"[15] and ignoring how different social, racial, political, and economic contexts might affect what a web of connection looks like. "Otherness" or difference is only dealt with on a very superficial level, one which acknowledges that the separate self of liberalism must be contextualized. Without an understanding of that context, however, the suggestion of the web replacing the ladder becomes a "corrective" to the prevailing mode of morality, a supplement meant to improve things, thereby avoiding a fundamental critique of that mode.[16]

Putting the context back into the liberal paradigm has been defended, at least in the case of women, as more than just adding woman's reality. The result of adding women is not simply a better fit between rights and reality but a radically transformed, potentially subversive right. For instance, when women assert their right to reproductive control, they reveal the important dimension of patriarchy that systematically oppresses women through control of reproduction. Further, staying within a rights paradigm has some important advantages. Karst reminds women that it enables us "to speak to men in language they understand."[17] Elizabeth Schneider notes how empowering rights language can be for women who have difficulty as a group believing in their own claims for justice.[18] Similar points are made by Robert Williams when he advises minority groups to take rights aggressively and to use them as primitive weapons loaded with myths until they "perfect new weapons out of the materials at hand provided by our insurrectionist discursive traditions."[19] All such suggestions carry, however, an implicit understanding of the *dangers* and limitations of rights thinking, even when rights thinking is improved to include context.

The difficulties of moving around in the liberal paradigm with a notion of group rights and an ethic of care are manifest both on a philosophical and practical plane. We still have to draw the limits on self (i.e., where self ends and community begins), and justice as fairness demands that we discover a way to evaluate the competing claims of groups and of individuals in groups. The problem of whether a Black woman should get a job ahead of a disabled woman or a Black man, or any such combination thereof, calls our attention to the competition inherent in justice as fairness. We are hard pressed in this instance to find the principles of justice that might enable us to rank these competing claims. The problem is particularly acute when all candidates are equally qualified, although the scenario is a somewhat abstract one given that a more common problem is the meaning of "qualified" itself. And given the requirement for abstract principles of justice, it becomes difficult to introduce ethical problems related to the real-life situation of these individuals in their respective groups.

Attempts to deal with competing groups on a practical level have been lame, at best. For instance, Larry May proposes that unorganized groups have priority (more rights) because their members can less easily escape the consequences of harm resulting from their group characteristic, a suggestion that leaves unanswered the questions who can be considered organized and what is harm. [20] A Canadian scholar, Leslie Armour, submits that we never consider an individual independent of her group, and never the group entirely at the peril of the individual. [21] Many feminists suggest that we determine whether or not a practice contributes to the disadvantage of the group and use this as our guide. [22] In effect, we look at the *result* of a practice on the group and ignore individual rights. [23] None of these prescriptions leave the judge or the human rights advocate much in the way of guidelines for concretely evaluating competing claims. We become embroiled in proving, measuring, and comparing disadvantage; these activities have always been fraught with peril for women and minorities whose realities, defined by their various group situations, are actively suppressed and even *inadmissible* in rights discourse and in the liberalism on which rights discourse is based.

The Postmodern Response [24]

Many of the intellectuals who reject the limits of liberalism and of a rights-based understanding of justice identify themselves as postmodern thinkers. The problems of speaking the unspeakable, revealing what has been suppressed, questioning the categories of truth, self, justice, and knowledge, preoccupy postmodernists whose reply to the problem of individual or group rights has been: let us not speak of rights at all because to do so is to stay locked into a framework which limits what we can know and say.

Jane Flax describes postmodernists as deconstructive "in that they seek to distance us from and make us sceptical about beliefs concerning truth, knowledge, power, the self, and language that are often taken for granted within, and serve as legitimation for contemporary Western culture."[25] Indeed, such beliefs form the core of scientific knowledge, knowledge that is privileged as legitimate knowledge in western culture. Rights thinking is heavily implicated in the postmodernist critique of scientific knowledge because it relies on the Enlightenment's beliefs in a stable, coherent, independent self; the primacy of reason over desire; and the notion of justice as an agreement between and among free individuals. Amended versions of rights concepts, the resort to group rights and to an ethic of care also fail to confront those very issues that postmodernists are most anxious about; namely, the definition of self and the notions of community, difference, and otherness.

Rational minds produce truth. Justice provides for the meeting of rational minds. What I say is true because I can prove it is. Referring to these essential items as an Enlightenment triad of beliefs, upon which liberals rely, Jean-François Lyotard has reflected that all postmodernists can be characterized by their "incredulity toward [these] metanarratives."[26] To replace the sweeping claims which Lyotard names metanarratives, postmodernists offer the notion of discourse.

For Michel Foucault, who has perhaps had the greatest impact among the postmodernists known in North America, discourse is the creation of meaning. Once we begin to focus on the deepest levels of where meaning is produced (i.e., in language), we come upon the rules that operate to suppress certain aspects of experience and highlight others. We discover that what we know is *produced* through these rules; that knowledge is simply one side of the coin while power, the power to regulate what is known, is the other. Discourse is the twin operation of power and knowledge and when we deconstruct scientific knowledge, for instance, we see that specific rules influence how we order our knowledge (experience) of the world.

The postmodern notion of discourse is wholly incompatible with the core beliefs of the Enlightenment, and thus with rights thinking, because it

contains the notion that knowledge is organized into particular configurations, patterns that are determined by power relations and not by individuals acting autonomously. In contrast, in rights thinking we use individual
reason to find the rules that govern rights. Legal reasoning, Joseph Singer
has written, is particularly dependent on rationality (and not, for example,
on intuition), confusing what is just with what is true, and assuming that
we can know, or at least agree on, what is true.[27] Singer and others also
point out that objectivity is still the god for those who embrace pluralism,
where various communities can have their own objectivity based on the
consensus they have achieved. The assumption is still that rational consensus is the source of all values and of knowing. Similarly Jean-François
Lyotard identifies the modern fiction that while there is no absolute truth,
the "people" get to decide what is true. The only way for the people to be
able to do so is through the mediation of knowledge; thus, "knowledge first
finds legitimacy within itself, and it is knowledge that is entitled to say what
the State and what Society are."[28]

When the field of study is Canadian law, as it is in this work, the postmodern critique of scientific knowledge and of the ideas of the Enlightenment
is especially helpful. Law embodies all of the central beliefs of the Enlightenment in a way that is immediately visible. It rests on the myth of objectivity based on man's innate rationalism. Its raison d'être is to *find* the rules
that can be used to arbitrate rights claims. In direct opposition to the
Enlightenment view of law is the postmodern perspective of law as discourse, which, as Zillah Eisenstein writes, means calling attention to "how
law establishes regulations, thoughts, and behavior and institutes expectations of what is legitimate and illegitimate behavior, what is acceptable and
unacceptable, what is criminal and legal, what is rational and irrational,
what is natural and unnatural."[29]

When women (and others) call attention to law as discourse, when they
demand, for instance, that judges "contextualize" and render decisions
that take into account their lived experience, the enormity and even the
absurdity of their demand should not deter us from recognizing its potential to seriously undermine the myths that buttress the law. A legal scholar,
in this case a man, who voices the opinion that "legal and moral questions
are matters to be answered by experience, emotion, introspection, and
conversation, rather than by logical proof"[30] may at first be laughed out of
court (or the scholarly journals); but, what happens when his words begin

to have an impact? Does this amount to insurrection? More significantly, what happens when that scholar, activist, or lawyer is a woman or a group of women?

Feminist Jurisprudence

Applying feminism to law fundamentally challenges the separation of reason from desire and the dichotomous way of thinking that falsely posits an objective rational truth as law's enterprise. Feminizing or contextualizing law requires confronting the boundaries between the self and community and coming to terms with the meaning of difference. Replete with difficulty and contradiction, it is a project that nevertheless offers a constructive response to those who fear that with the dethroning of objectivity and truth there can be no meaningful way to decide how to live a good life. Feminism applied to law insists on law's transformative potential, that is, on the role that law can play in the creation of a society based on an ethic that responds to needs, honours difference, and rejects the abstractions of scientific discourse.

Women have been wary of equality games ever since they began playing them in courts of law in the early 1900s. In a forum where differences between individuals in their communities are denied, it has always been difficult to introduce women's gender-based realities. Women noticed,[31] for instance, that in the absence of an understanding of individuals in their various communities, courts confronted with the task of evaluating competing claims of individuals relied on the notion that likes must be treated alike: all women must be treated the same; all men must be treated the same. In practice, this approach meant it was often possible to argue that women were not entitled to be treated as men because they were not comparable to men; there were demonstrable biological and social differences. Women met this impasse whenever they got into court. Those who wanted the right to be lawyers were told that as wives and mothers, they *were not like* men, that is, they were not similarly situated to men, and so did not have the right to equal treatment in this area. A first step toward equal treatment was achieved when women sought recognition for being persons. They won that right conditionally in 1929; the Privy Council ruled that the word person, *depending on the context,* may include women.[32]

By the 1980s enough women were involved in the practice of law to begin theorizing publicly about their experiences. The question that inevitably suggested itself, given the widespread application of such concepts as likes must be treated alike or similar situation, was whether or not the master's tools could ever be used to dismantle the master's house. Journals of feminist jurisprudence,[33] a phenomenon of the 1980s, all published articles that sought to respond to this question.

An early response, often associated with the American legal theorist Wendy Williams,[34] was to play the equality game as best one could, insisting on women's fundamental sameness to men. Williams saw that game as one played with loaded dice. The analytical key to most legal judgements, she wrote, was clearly still the concept of similarly situated; the "rule" that if men and women are similarly situated with respect to the purposes of the law in question, then they were to be treated equally. Since the analysis always turned on stereotypes of men's and women's roles in society, and since points of strict comparison were difficult to find, it was relatively easy for a court to conclude that women were differently situated and therefore could be treated in a different way. Believing that legal equality was of some importance to women, Williams opted to play the court game by giving judges as little opportunity as possible to invoke the stereotypes she felt they all shared. This meant never claiming special or sex-based treatment. Thus, for example, women would not argue for pregnancy leave based on their biological needs; instead, they would make a claim on the more neutral ground of disability.

To claim special needs placed women at risk because they were then automatically deemed not similarly situated to men. Moreover, the special-needs route enabled courts to focus exclusively on women's difference without evaluating other factors, such as employers' responsibilities to provide disability leave for all workers. Indeed, Williams feared that employers would not hire women if forced to recognize their different needs. In later articles Williams would be more explicit about the basis for her views, arguing that courts were structured to view the task of equality as one requiring a comparison of women to men, and that owning up to sex differences was "sheer folly."[35] She was prepared, however, to find ways of meeting women's needs within the framework of comparison, suggesting for example that any special benefits women needed should also be extended to men.

Ann Scales[36] articulated the opposite position to Williams's, although both (at this time) saw the need to play the game under the given rules, and both were under no illusions about its dangers for women. Scales argued that recognizing women's special needs as they related to pregnancy and breastfeeding was not a claim for special treatment or a claim to be "taken into account," but rather a claim *not* to be taken into account in a degrading way. In effect, it was a claim for equal treatment. Elizabeth Wolgast elaborated much the same approach as Scales, making the distinction between equal rights and special rights and arguing that equality required the recognition of both.[37]

Pregnancy, as Marie Ashe has commented, effectively "blows away" the logic of the similarly situated rule, emphasizing women's difference and forcing those who seek to accommodate it within the rule of similarly situated to resort to extensive manipulation of language and concepts, determining, for instance, to what extent differences are biological and to what extent social.[38] Feminists who saw the difficulties in both Scales and Williams's approaches, and who, such as Catharine MacKinnon resisted the similarly situated rule, took the risk of failing to convince the courts to respond to women's needs.

Indeed, feminist legal scholars, troubled by the constricting features of the discourse in which they were obliged to work, often wondered, as Anne Simon did, if women were "doing something not really worth doing" when they focused on making better arguments and translating their reality into a legal framework. The process of translation narrowed the issue under consideration and limited the transformative potential so critical to a feminist approach. To use Anne Simon's example, when the issue of armed combat is taken into court on an equality model, the issue becomes whether or not women, excluded from such combat, are being treated equally. There is no space for introducing the feminist issue of opposition to militarism.[39] Clearly, getting the legal system to work for women would require more than a reworking of old concepts.

Beyond "Likes Must be Treated Alike"

In 1980, Janet Rifkin ended one of the first articles to explicitly take up the question of law and patriarchy by stating that "the paradigm of law as a symbol of male authority has not been challenged."[40] Seven years later, Christine Littleton's article directed that challenge by proposing that "feminists cannot ignore the concrete experience of women"; it is that experience that must guide how they assessed the law and what they wanted to gain from it.[41] This has certainly been the hallmark of feminist jurisprudence, but in the intervening years between Rifkin and Littleton, many feminists found that taking the concrete experience of women into the courtroom meant explaining what individual men or the system of male dominance or both *did* to women. It became clear that gender hierarchy and not gender difference was at issue, although feminists working in law continued utilizing both concepts.

One strategy emphasizing women's experience that emerged from feminist legal work was to flood the courts with women's stories in order to get, in the words of Robin West, "one simple point across: men's narrative story and phenomenological description of law is not women's story and phenomenology of the law." If women's values were recognized, she wisely added, "all hell would not break loose"; in fact, the world would be a better place.[42] Another feminist lawyer described such a world as one where decisions are made according to what's right under the circumstances, although such a society would not in fact be pluralist but feminist in the sense of having a definite vision of the good life.[43]

Ambitious and brave in its vision, the project of feminism applied to law, as Robin West and others describe it, is nonetheless troubling in its assumption that women's stories and careful crafting will in fact do the trick. The category of "women's experience" is a highly problematic one that unconsciously sets up a dichotomy of women and men. It is a "cruel irony," as Denise Riley has phrased it, that "the more that the category of woman is asserted, whether glowingly moral or unjustly accused, or as a sexual species fully apart, the more its apparent remoteness from 'humanity' is underwritten."[44] More significant, perhaps, is the often unacknowledged universalism concealed in the phrase "women's experience." While a universal female experience may be necessary as a question of strategy in a court of law, given law's insistence on categorical claims, there is considerable risk that the description of female experience will express only the realities of women from dominant groups. The claim that femaleness has a universal meaning, Trinh Minh-ha reminds us, sets up ethnicity against womanhood, "as if woman can never be ethnic."[45]

Canadian Feminism Applied to Law

Getting men to listen to women's stories is in fact a major preoccupation for those Canadian scholars whose work is marked by a keen appreciation of how legal discourse silences women's voices. Indulging in a bit of fantasy, Christine Boyle described how a feminist judge, relying on the feminist method of consciousness-raising, would listen to women, comparing and analyzing their experience of the world to her own. The approach may border on fantasy but, as Boyle noted, lawyers usually do try to appeal to a shared perception of the world when they speak to judges. Since men and women, or women and judges, tend not to have that shared perception, women have to work doubly hard to arrive at a shared understanding of reality. Boyle guessed that this entailed "making complex factual arguments about patterns and results of discrimination," a task she takes on in the area of sexual assault.[46]

One difficulty in presenting women's stories in court is the legal practice of grounding an issue solely in the particular material facts of the case. Thus, women have to first show how their membership in the group women materially affects the issue at hand. In a rape trial for example, as Boyle noted, gender is a material fact since society eroticizes female lack of consent in the sexual act, and this has considerable bearing on where the dividing line between rape and sexual intercourse is placed.[47]

Introducing gender considerations is no easy task, however, given legal and Enlightenment values of empirical proof. As Boyle explained it: "The idea is to help decision-makers hear women describe their own experience. The reality is that this experience has to be made credible by an expert describing conditions which may then become rigid requirements in their own rights."[48] Proof that is dependent on empirical validation is incompatible with the telling of personal stories, stories that may require a narrative rather than a scientific mode and where the social and historical context of the tale is critical to our understanding of it.

In the landscape of Canadian legal feminism, Shelley Gavigan is one scholar who turned to the postmodern notion of discourse to relieve the weight of the implications of deconstruction. Historically, Gavigan notes, feminists have been led astray by adopting a perspective that law has its own central and autonomous importance, rather than adopting a view that it is a form of social control *integrally connected* to other institutions. In rape law reform efforts of the early 1970s, for example, feminists focused on the sexism of law and sought to make it gender neutral with the change in terminology from rape to sexual assault. The strategy backfired when the issue of spousal assault came to be considered a few years later because a gender-neutral framework could not capture the reality of how women as a group are specifically at risk and are harmed by rape.[49] As Catharine MacKinnon has also said, there are considerable perils in viewing rape as anything other than a sex crime. The same is true of wife assault, a crime that cannot be understood unless the gender identities of victim and aggressor are taken into account as "material facts."

For Gavigan, a more fruitful approach to law is to go beyond seeing it as an isolated form of control, where reform represents either "a tightening of the mesh" or a "widening of the net," and look instead for how a particular practice reproduced a particular set of circumstances in a particular historical context. That is, if we focus on how law perpetuates or contributes to women's subordination, we can better see how it might also do the opposite. Thus, reform may at times serve women, at others not. In the case of abortion rights, for example, courts have not uniformly rejected the notion that women have a right to choose whether or not to bear children; there have been cracks through which women have been able to advance their interests.[50]

Mary O'Brien and Shiela McIntyre are two feminists who agree with Gavigan on the point of looking for the cracks in law. Rejecting a straightforward explanation of hegemony for the way law operates, they too see transformative potential in the search for the points where "women's specifically female consciousness in so male a culture" might have "counter-hegemonic impact."[51]

Canadian women's search for ways to present their reality in court and be heard became considerably more directed and intense with the Charter of Rights and Freedoms. It is to this story that we can now turn, having explored the theoretical challenges of applying feminism to law.

❖

CHAPTER ONE

FROM LOBBYING TO LEGAL ACTION:
CHANGING THE MEANING OF EQUALITY, 1970-1985

B ETWEEN 1970 and 1985, perhaps more so than at any other time previously, Canadians talked a great deal about the right to equality. In 1970, the release of the *Report of the Royal Commission on the Status of Women* spawned a good deal of organizing around equality issues. By the late 1970s, the unresolved problems originating in the bad "fit" of lived experience into the rights mould, flowed to the forefront, prompting those who worked in the rights field to attempt to expand the mould itself. In 1980, the federal government's initiative to patriate Canada's constitution, adding to it a Charter of Rights and Freedoms, triggered a public airing of the meaning of rights. As part of the contemporary debate, a small group of legally-trained women began to express public concern over the relevance of proposed Charter definitions of equality to women's lives. In 1985, some of these women created the women's Legal Education and Action Fund as an attempt to connect the rhetoric of equality with the reality.

The Pre-Charter Context

The year 1970, a point of departure for many historians of the post-war Canadian feminist movement, is the year that the Royal Commission on the Status of Women (RCSW) issued its *Report:* "an official public event [that] clearly defined the status of Canadian women as a social problem *warranting treatment.*"[1] In keeping with the tenor of submissions received, the Commission's *Report* defined equality as freedom from discrimination and stressed "the principle that permits no distinctions in rights and freedoms between men and women."[2] Emphasizing women's economic independence and right to participate equally in the public sphere, the *Report* was categoric on the point that equality required "in certain areas for an interim period ... special treatment to overcome the adverse effects of discriminatory practices."[3] Further, it identified the demands of maternity as central to barriers keeping women from full economic independence and urged the government to take into account women's needs in this area.

Despite its departure from a paradigm of strict equality (equality as identical treatment), the RCSW's *Report* was conspicuous for its emphasis on individual women and its lack of self-consciousness about the group and systemic nature of women's situation. Indeed, the *Report* illustrates what Jill Vickers has identified as the classical concept of liberalism – fair play and the notion of equal opportunity for individuals. Fair play, Vickers notes, is to be distinguished from the liberal concept of fair shares: the notion that society has an obligation to redistribute its burdens and benefits more equitably among all its members.[4]

In the decade launched by the RCSW's *Report,* fair play continued to compete with fair shares as a way of understanding and solving inequality. Although there were areas, and the court was one of them, where the fair-play approach dominated, elsewhere there was a growing recognition that the formal, individual right to equal treatment was an inadequate response to the phenomenon of inequality. For instance, William Black has written about the evolution in human rights legislation in the 1970s from the understanding that human rights laws were violated only when there was a (provable) intent to discriminate to the concept of unintentional discrimination. Unintentional discrimination contained within it the notion that certain practices affected groups adversely with the result that they did not enjoy their fair share of society's resources.[5] The trend began with women's equal pay claims which highlighted the absence of individual intent but the very real presence, nonetheless, of a discriminatory situation. By 1977, when a Sikh security guard complained that the requirement that he replace his turban (a religious requirement) by a company cap unjustly discriminated against him on the basis of his religion, a human rights board of inquiry found that, while there was no intent to discriminate against Sikhs, the policy did have the impact of denying them equal employment opportunities.[6]

Women and the Charter

The story of Canadian women and the Charter enables us to see where the fair-shares approach led women in the 1980s. The patriation of Canada's constitution from Britain had long been on the political agenda; but in the late 1970s, when the people of Quebec elected a provincial government committed to taking that province out of Confederation, the issue suddenly seemed urgent. In November of 1978 and February of 1979, two conferences of first ministers were held on constitutional issues. Neither paid much attention to women's (or, for that matter, Native peoples') rights in law. Indeed, so complete was the omission that when the February conference concluded with a draft of proposals that would transfer jurisdiction over family law from the federal government to the provinces, there was no thought spared for the impact such a transfer would have on women.[7] The next conference of first ministers was held in September 1980. By that time, women in a position to have information about the proposed changes and who were aware of the problems over the transfer of jurisdiction on divorce law were on full alert.

Throughout the summer of 1980, the Canadian Advisory Council on the Status of Women (CACSW), headed by Doris Anderson, former editor of *Chatelaine* magazine and a well-known feminist and Liberal, researched the constitution issue in preparation for a conference in September. The National Action Committee on the Status of Women (NAC) declared in its May/June memo that constitutional reform would be its priority for the year.[8] NAC and CACSW's summer activities around the constitution cannot be said to have amounted to popular feminist concern; but, both the content of their response to the government's proposal to entrench a Charter of Rights and Freedoms and the process through which their concerns ultimately reached Canadian women at large tell us a great deal about how equality was understood and acted upon by these women.

Beverly Baines, a law professor, was commissioned by the CACSW to research its position on the equality clauses of the proposed Charter of Rights and Freedoms. Her work, "Women, Human Rights and the Constitution,"[9] later became the brief the CACSW presented to the Special Joint Senate Subcommittee appointed to hear responses to the proposed Charter. It would also become the working document of the women's lobby for constitutional change. Besides its historical importance, Baines's paper is an admirably succinct explanation of the meaning of equality then being espoused.

"Women, Human Rights and the Constitution" began by clarifying its use of the term human rights, indicating its author's awareness of the limitations of the paradigm with which she was asked to work:

> When expressed in traditional human rights terminology, the convention has arisen that women's claims for personhood are treated as claims for equality. The equality approach is based on female-to-male comparisons. There is always a risk that comparisons will not produce a concept of legal personhood which is founded on the Royal Commission's principle of a common status of men and women.... The equality approach could produce more immediate results, which hopefully would serve as the basis for an acceptable, if not utopian, personhood.[10]

Implicit in this statement, and evident elsewhere in the article when Baines examined Supreme Court decisions on equality issues, is the fear that the process of comparing men and women usually resulted in men being taken as the norm. Women would later in the decade make an argument for the norm having to shift, but the framework of rights discourse and the notion of equality make comparison implicit; in this paradigm, restructuring of the roles men and women play becomes virtually impossible.[11]

During the 1970s, the Supreme Court of Canada produced ten decisions involving equality before the law (the phrase of the Canadian Bill of Rights); nine out of the ten decisions concluded that there had been no inequality. Pointing this out in her paper, Baines noted that in the interest of equality we needed to replace either the Bill of Rights or the judges, or both, and that we ignored at our peril "the specific material interest" men have in the oppression of women. [12] In 1980, as now, this position required a good deal of courage, even the more so since it had come out under the auspices of the governmental CACSW.

In Baines's view the dismal record of the Supreme Court revealed that equality before the law was by no means a self-evident principle and required the intervention of other principles to give it substance. One of these other principles had effectively worked against women's interests in the cases of Jeannette Lavell and Stella Bliss. Lavell, an Indian woman, claimed that Section 12(1b) of the Indian Act, which stripped her of her Indian status upon marriage to a non-Indian (and did not strip Indian men who married non-Indians), was discriminatory. Bliss argued that unemployment insurance policies requiring pregnant women to have worked a longer qualifying period than other unemployed workers before qualifying for benefits were discriminatory. The operative principle used by the court was the "rule of law." Essentially, parliament made the law, probably for valid reasons, and everyone was subject to it, regardless of personal circumstance. Both Jeannette Lavell and Stella Bliss maintained that the law excluded them or treated them unequally; they did not argue that they ought not to be bound by the law. In other words, the law itself was unjust. The judges, however, without benefit of a constitution that would enable them to evaluate state actions, were bound to the letter of the law and assessed its intent and how it worked in the specific cases under consideration.

In *Bliss,* The Honourable Mr Justice Pratte employed the principle of "relevant distinction," that is, there must be a logical connection between the distinction made, in this case pregnancy, and the consequences that flowed from it, denial of unemployment benefits. He reasoned that since pregnancy was (in his view) a voluntary condition, and since the government very reasonably did not want pregnant women to work, a special benefit scheme, different from the regular one available to workers, was in order. Presumably, women had no basis on which to protest its inequality; it was a gift anyway! A similar reasoning was at work with the principle of "valid government objective"; that is, validity was to be assessed in terms of the logical connection between the distinction and the consequences. In effect, as Baines argued: "Since governments can give reasons for virtually all their legislation, the effect of linking inequality to irrelevance is that inequality will be defined out of the courts while still existing in real life."[13]

To "stop these holes" in law,[14] Baines emphasized that the proposed Charter had to send a clear signal to the courts that Canadians held dearly the principle of equality between the sexes. Further, equality connoted both negative rights (the right to be free from discrimination, for example) and positive rights (the right to enjoy a fair share of society's benefits). Because the court often resorted to other principles to give equality meaning, Baines also wanted the purpose of the equality value to be clear. She described this purpose as

> 'evening-up' the legal status of a disadvantaged group relative to an advantaged group [which] means that the laws must not classify on the basis of the characteristic of the disadvantaged group unless that disadvantaged group (not the courts, not the advantaged group, and not the government) is prepared to agree that such classification is necessary for that process.[15]

As evening-up suggests, judges were being called upon to make decisions with an eye to their impact on the status of disadvantaged groups, a type of jurisprudence Marc Gold has termed "result-oriented jurisprudence."[16] Result-oriented equality was very much built on the assumption that the law is used to redistribute the burdens and benefits of living in Canada, a fair-shares approach to justice.

As the Baines paper suggested, women working in the legal area were clear that the new Charter had to convey the importance of equality between the sexes. In the normal course of things, their position would have been expressed in briefs and papers and lobbied for on Parliament Hill. The government would then have responded according to its perception of the level of support for such sentiments. Perhaps resistance would not have been great, given the evolution in thinking in the legal community and elsewhere from classical liberalism to a fair-shares approach and public awareness of the outcome of cases like *Bliss* and *Lavell*. That the course of events did not in fact run as smoothly is an indication of how little women can take for granted when we assert our interests collectively.

Rosemary Billings, one of the key activists who organized the women's lobby to change the constitution, writes in her introduction to Penney Kome's book on the lobby [17] that there appeared to have been three stages of women's involvement in the constitution. Before December 1980, the lobby involved mainly women knowledgeable in law and drawn from the established women's organizations; this was followed by a middle phase, that of the Ad Hoc Committee of Women on the Constitution, which attracted a wider following; during a final phase the issue reverted to the "legally-expert elite." [18]

The women who initiated constitutional lobbying were from the feminist sector often described as mainstream or institutionalized feminism, the sector in which well-established national women's groups engage in lobbying for reform of existing social institutions. It is highly likely that they shared those social and political perspectives which permitted "a shared realm of discourse." [19] What is certain from their subsequent organizing is that they were able to tap the communities of their various organizations and that they were well-versed in and comfortable with the politics of lobbying. They were, in all probability, women who, like the women Christine Appelle surveyed from NAC, "trust[ed] in the political system to bring about change and [who] show[ed] a desire to partake in the existing political structure," [20] but were nonetheless personally confronted by the contradiction that as women that system did not work for them.

Charter activists recruited women through networks they knew and trusted. Lynda Ryan-Nye, one of the leading figures on the committee, recalled that the networks of the Canadian Research Institute for the Advancement of Women (CRIAW), NAC, and the National Association of Women and the Law (NAWL) were all activated, as were those of the older and more traditional women's groups such as the Canadian Federation of University Women. [21] Other women, coming out of a background of professional concern with rights issues, joined the Ad Hoc Committee on their own initiative. For instance, Marilou McPhedran, who later became one of the founders of LEAF, remembers that she had just started a research contract on international human rights statutes and joined the Committee when Doris Anderson resigned from her job over the government's cancellation of a conference on women and the proposed Charter scheduled for February 14th 1981. Mary Eberts, another founder of LEAF, worked under contract for the CACSW when it commissioned several papers on women and the constitution during the summer of 1980. While she did not play a direct role in the lobby, she was one of several Canadian women with the legal awareness to know that the February 14th conference was the women's voice the government had so far tried to silence. Other women later involved in LEAF, Beth Atcheson and Beth Symes, became involved in the women's lobby after the government-sponsored CACSW conference took place in May of 1981. [22]

Putting together their own conference to replace the cancelled one, the newly formed Ad Hoc Committee of Women on the Constitution tackled head on the inadequacies of the proposed Charter. In proceedings that would have seemed formal and intimidating to women less acquainted with parliamentary procedures and *Robert's Rules of Order,* they hammered out resolutions to take to the government of Canada. They resolved that there should be no Charter of Rights and Freedoms unless it included appropriate equality guarantees. Further, the Charter should begin with the strong statement that the rights and freedoms set out within it were guaranteed equally to men and women with no limitations. It was this statement that became Clause 28, an equality guarantee few women elsewhere in the world have won in law. Other conference resolutions sought to tighten up the Charter's clauses to reflect the strength of women's equality claim. For instance, conference participants agreed that Section 15 on equality rights should make it clear that equality referred to equality under the law, in law (i.e., in its application), and to the equal protection and benefit of the law, phrases meant to convey the importance of considering the impact of a law on women. They also stressed that Clause 27 on multicultural rights should not contain a loophole that would enable cultural communities to discriminate against women in the name of cultural preservation. Here the *Lavell* case clearly influenced their demands. Finally, women insisted on the use of the word person, fearing that the use of the word "everyone" would result in women's claims being weighed against those of a foetus in cases involving reproductive rights.

The Charter activists' efforts paid off. In 1982, Canadian women could boast, as few of our sisters elsewhere could, that we enjoyed a strong constitutional guarantee of equality. Section 28 of the Charter of Rights and

Freedoms contained the resounding declaration that "notwithstanding anything in this Charter, the rights and freedoms referred to in it are guaranteed equally to male and female persons."[23] What such a guarantee might mean in practice remained for most Canadian women a mystery. Section 15, containing specific guarantees of sex equality, namely, that every individual "is equal before and under the law and has the right to the equal benefit and protection of the law" without discrimination on the basis of sex, was only slightly clearer.

It was a victory that left in its wake a trail of bitterness. Jill Vickers has suggested that the women's groups who supported the Charter and were involved in the lobby were those who realised that the loss of firm equality guarantees would have been "a devastating symbolic blow."[24] Indeed one of the Ad Hoc women, Linda Ryan-Nye, declared that while the constitutional guarantee of equality between men and women was "a helluva lot to lose, it was not a helluva lot to gain."[25] Rosemary Billings, another activist, felt that the lobby enabled women to experience the contradiction between their perception of having equal status and the concrete experience gained during the lobby of having legislators pay scant attention to them. Indeed, while the lobby remained largely an initiative of the institutionalized feminist sector, drawing on middle-class white professional women who believed in the political process, most of the participants experienced in a personal way the marginal status they occupied in Canadian society. When the popular phase of the constitutional lobbying was over, and professional, legally trained women once again took up the issue on their own, the lessons would not be forgotten. Their faith in the system would continue unshaken but beside it was a growing sex-consciousness, of the necessity and meaning of organizing for women's interests autonomously.

Constitutional lobbying served the function of enabling women to articulate precisely their vision of equality. The vision of fair shares, while not unique to women, nonetheless became so refined during discussions about the Charter that women, at least the professional legal elite, could continue to build on the lobby once the Charter was a reality and prepare for the next phase of charterwatching and litigation armed with a precise notion of what equality meant and how they wanted to secure it through the law.

Charterwatching

Rights on paper mean nothing unless the courts correctly interpret their scope and application. Charter activists began trying to influence judicial interpretation through charterwatching, an all-consuming activity. It entailed having national consultations, planning conferences, writing books and articles, making speeches, doing audits of statutes, offering workshops; in short, attempting to inform the decision-makers, women, and the Canadian public (in that order) exactly what the new equality guarantees should mean in law.

The frenzy of activities began, as though by a starter's gun, when the government included in its constitution bill a three-year moratorium on Section 15's equality rights. Ostensibly giving governments sufficient time to bring their legislation into conformity with the law, the delay inspired women to plan for the day when they could take their unresolved equality claims to court, armed with the hard-won guarantees of Sections 15 and 28.

Not surprisingly, the women most compelled to plan for litigation and to charterwatch were those legally-trained or connected to the women's organizations active on the lobby. As early as March 1981, Marilou McPhedran recorded in her diary her awareness of the experience of American women's legal defence funds and their possible relevance to the Canadian context.[26] In May 1981, when the long-delayed CACSW conference on Women and the Constitution took place in Ottawa, Beth Atcheson, later a founder of LEAF, mentioned the idea of a Canadian women's litigation fund in her speech, which she had prepared in collaboration with Beth Symes and Marilou McPhedran.[27] Mary Eberts, the chair of the conference, Beth Symes, and Beth Atcheson were then commissioned by the CACSW to work with the researcher Jennifer Stoddart on a feasibility study of a women's litigation fund. Although the study, *Women and Legal Action*, was not available until the fall of 1984, its authors relied on its findings to start organizing support for the idea in 1982.[28]

In charterwatching, it became evident that a disagreeable theme running through the organizing efforts around Section 15 was the sharp difference in opinions between male experts on the Charter and women with a knowledge of the Charter. This gender gap began with the betrayal of women during the November 1981 lobby over the issue of who could opt out of the equality clauses.

Beth Atcheson recalled that during the lobby the press quoted extensively the opinions of male Charter experts who, among other things, pronounced that the opting-out clause, Section 33, was in fact a good compromise because it secured for women a stronger Section 15 at the price of the remote possibility that a province would opt out of being bound by it. Unimpressed by the provinces' record on women's rights, many of the women who worked on constitutional issues rejected the views of the most widely-quoted male experts: Gordon Fairweather, chief commissioner of the Canadian Human Rights Commission; Alan Borovoy, counsel for the Canadian Civil Liberties Association; and Walter Tarnopolsky, a legal expert who was later appointed to the Ontario Supreme Court. Nicknamed the three kings, Beth Atcheson remembered the Charter women's general sentiment towards these men: "There was a great deal of anger that there was no reason why we couldn't know as much about the Charter as they knew and [that] we couldn't also be taking a public position."[29] At times, the male experts' point of view on the Charter seemed to have ignored the entire history of the women's constitutional lobby, or, at the very least, missed some of the finer legal points it expressed. For instance, in January 1982 the *Calgary Herald* quoted Tarnopolsky as saying, "Surely 'everyone' includes women. I don't really see the need for this (extra) provision."[30] Women's historical difficulty in winning acceptance for the idea that general terms such as the word "everyone" and the word "persons" included both men and women, and their fear that everyone would also include foetuses, clearly did not influence his perception of Charter issues.

In May 1982, when their anger had simmered through meetings of the National Association of Women and the Law and NAC's constitutional committee, several of the women connected to the issue applied for funding and organized a national think tank which was held in Toronto. They invited well-known constitutional expert Peter Hogg and Walter Tarnopolsky because, not only were they trying to secure answers to their questions about what the constitutional equality guarantees meant, they were beginning to adopt what they described as a process of "influencing the influencers," an approach fuelled by their increasing awareness that "things were being written that we didn't exactly agree with."[31] A number of ideas surfaced at this time about how best to promote women's interests in law: the idea of a defence fund was already on the table and to this was added the idea of a legal text book and a symposium, all based on the belief that "it was very important to get in at the academic level."[32]

In their own educational session, billed as a workshop on the Charter and held in the same month as the think tank, the women proceeded to determine what their position was on the new law. As a first effort, "a sort of boot strap thing" as Beth Symes described it, women assembled their expertise and found that among the twenty-four or more presenters they did in fact have their own response to the three kings. By summer, some began work on the symposium, while others continued their research and writing. Again, the rationale was the same: if women could convey their point of view to those in "responsible positions,"[33] they could influence how equality rights were ultimately understood in the courts.

Energetic in their efforts to promote women's constitutional interests, a core of women in Toronto, who were active on constitutional issues, created a trust fund known as the Charter of Rights Educational Fund (CREF), a Charter of Rights Coalition (CORC), and called together thirty women in the area who launched several educational activities. The minutes of the meeting held on November 25, 1982, at the large and prestigious law firm of Tory, Tory (where Mary Eberts worked) indicated a general consensus on the need to publicize the issues and further educate women on the specifics of the equality guarantees. Under the auspices of CREF, two study days were planned and, at a later meeting, a committee was struck to co-ordinate the massive undertaking of an audit of federal and provincial statutes not in compliance with the Charter. The idea of a legal defence fund, supported very strongly by the group's only independently wealthy member Nancy Jackman, is described in the minutes as the "least formalized" of all the projects.[34]

The study days, held on January 15 and February 19, 1983, attracted over 170 persons,[35] largely women from the legal community. The papers presented, and which were later published, made clear that the group saw their task as one of shaping the legal community's views, and the judiciary's in particular, on the meaning of equality. For example, in her presentation

Beth Atcheson stressed the difference between equality and non-discrimination rights:

> To speak in terms of non-discrimination or disadvantaged (as in sub-section 15(2)) is to assume that, in whatever factual situation, there is a situation which is accepted as the norm. The question then becomes one of moving a party to that norm. What happens when the difference between the two parties is not seen as adverse? What happens when you cannot compare the situation of opposites, that is men and women?[36]

Her colleague Katherine Swinton supplied the answer: "Women have to be ready to prove to the courts that a particular piece of legislation is based on a policy of differentiation between the sexes which is illegitimate."[37] Subsequent speakers went on to discuss how this might be done. American legal experts shared their experience with non-discrimination legislation, warning Canadian women where the pitfalls lay. Section 28, it was conceded, gave Canadian women an advantage their American sisters did not have: "an independently negotiated agreement between parliamentarians and Canada's women" that gender-based discrimination was to be taken seriously.[38]

The statute audit project, born "out of the nasty suspicion that their [the government's] idea of equality and ours was not going to be the same,"[39] intended to pinpoint for Canadian legislatures exactly what had to be done to avoid subsequent legal battles over equality; but, it was also meant to provide women with a "catalogue" of changes from which they might launch a litigation effort. The Americans, with whom the CACSW's *Women and Legal Action* team had spoken, had generally concurred that litigation had to be staged and to do so required a clear knowledge of the range of laws that discriminated against women. The seventy women who worked on the audit were organized into teams and co-ordinated by a CREF member. They began on the premise that equality means "more to women than the equal opportunity to participate in a male-defined world."[40] They then examined ten areas of women's lives, suggesting where and how the law had contributed to a situation of inequality. Key to their approach was the notion that "the aim is not to sex-neutralize all laws and pretend that one has thereby created equality: the aim is to positively accommodate sex specific situations."[41]

While both the audit and the study days dealt with the complexities of using the equality guarantees in litigation, the activities of the Charter of Rights Coalition were more broad-based in appeal. A key figure behind CORC's creation was Pat Hacker who, during her lobbying for Section 28 and later when she served as chair of NAC's constitutional committee, was concerned that Canadian women had to be made aware of the three-year moratorium and of the need to push governments into action before this time was up. As a result, NAC created CORC as a subcommittee of its constitutional committee. Made up of Nancy Jackman, Lee Grills, and Janka Seydegart, this team called together representatives from NAC, the Canadian Council of Learning Opportunities for Women (CCLOW), the Elizabeth Fry Society, the Canadian Federation of Business and Professional Women's Clubs, Energy Probe, Voice of Women, and the Women's Unit of the Anglican Church of Canada. Conspicuous by their absence were women from local, less-established groups, of the non-institutionalized feminist sector.

The CORC group received government funding to plan a national conference on Charter issues that would complement the symposium then being planned "for legal types." Nancy Jackman, who led the CORC team, remembered that they then began to build a series of "mini-coalitions" across the country, using the institutionalized women's groups as a base. The function of these coalitions was to "bug" their governments about the moratorium and educate women about the Charter. CORC prepared a slide tape show and an educational kit which optimistically declared:

> There is potential in the Charter of Rights to support whatever change women want. It's like a magic wand one could wave to bring about things like fair labour legislation, better protection for women in areas such as sexual assault and enactment of affirmative action programs. *Women can get what we want if we lobby now and do our research and help judges understand what equality means.*[42] (emphasis added)

The idea of a national conference, however, proved unworkable given the difficulties of Quebec women's groups with the Charter issue. The CORC group settled for a series of regional task forces and conferences, thereby facilitating the development of regional bases – in B.C., for example, where CORC women later formed the West Coast LEAF – and providing an opportunity for women from Toronto and Ottawa to travel the country and organize a litigation fund. [43]

The Charterwatchers

Who were the women who worked so devotedly to protect the constitutional interests of the women of Canada? There were remarkable continuity and overlap between the groups active during the lobby and CREF, CORC, and other committees struck by the institutionalized women's groups on related Charter issues. As Nancy Jackman remarked in an interview: "The charterwatchers are the charterwatchers. We go in and out of different groups. When Ad Hoc needs to be ginned up, we gin it up. For CREF and CORC, the same thing applies."[44] Her perspective is shared by the others. Beth Atcheson and Beth Symes jokingly recalled during the round table discussion on the history of LEAF that, although on paper there were a number of CORC committees, for a long time they were the only two women in it.

A quick survey of the major projects undertaken during the years of charterwatching reveals the same names on the lists of initiators. Beth Atcheson, Beth Symes, and Mary Eberts formed the *Women and Legal Action* team; they were also on the statute audit committee, were key presenters during the study days and at the Toronto city hall workshop, wrote legal articles, and participated in a number of educational forums. Mary Eberts eventually co-edited the major textbook on women and the Charter, *Equality Rights and the Canadian Charter of Rights and Freedoms.*[45] Marilou McPhedran's name heads most lists, a level of activism recognized by the Canadian government when it presented to her the Order of Canada for her role in the women's constitutional lobby. She organized the city hall workshop in May 1981 and was often the one cited in minutes of meetings as responsible for such activities as securing grants and co-ordinating the recruitment of women. Similarly, Nancy Jackman began her Charter activism when Kay McPherson invited her to join NAC, playing a key role in co-ordinating CORC's activities and in the founding of LEAF. (All five women were central figures in the formation of LEAF.) A measure of the central role played in the period between 1980 and 1985 is the fact that the meetings of CREF, CORC, and other projects usually took place at the Toronto law firms where they worked. Other women, such as Magda Seydegart, Lynn Smith, and Denise Arsenault, found themselves drawn into a network of related activities at various intervals.

The small "Toronto core" (a term they themselves have used in interviews) led a national group of women who shared similar social and professional backgrounds as well as institutional and professional connections. The media called them "sleek professional women of the big cities,"[46] while those who attended their events sometimes agreed, often self-critically describing themselves as "women lawyers in very expensive suits ... we speak with assurance, hire nannies for our children, and learn the rules of 'power dressing' in our first years of practice."[47] These activists, whose very serious commitment is trivialized by the media and by their own self-description, represented a small, relatively homogeneous core (all were white middle-class professionals) who activated a network of similarly-situated women. When Marilou McPhedran planned the city hall workshop, she looked for women who could be described as well-known, conscientious, academics, public speakers, and bilingual[48] – qualities that certainly limited who could be drawn into this type of activity. Of course, the activity itself inhibited the participation of women from diverse backgrounds. The twenty-four women whose names appeared on the agenda of the workshop, and who had been asked to submit their résumés to the organizing committee, were outstanding legal scholars whose careers in law-related fields already showed signs of the exceptional. Many LEAF women came from this group.[49]

The homogeneity of these Charter activists meant that they possessed a number of skills and resources particularly suited to the tasks they assumed. Mary Eberts, commenting on those who would later form LEAF, noted wryly that they consisted of women who had "all chosen to be marginal in roughly the same place," that is, in the largest and most prestigious of the city's law firms.[50] They had at their disposal, therefore, the tremendous resources of these firms which were utilized, whenever they could be, throughout the years of charterwatching and of LEAF's formation. A professional legal connection to women's issues and to women's legal equality meant that they also shared a common base of knowledge. Further, they were well-versed in the arts of grant applications and thoroughly familiar with working the corridors of power.

Equally significant in the self-portrait of the Toronto core is their identification with feminism. Speaking of the "strong connections" between and among them, Beth Atcheson recalled that previous to their charterwatching activism they had worked collectively on a feminist project and, by the time the Charter issue came up, they were "out of the closet" as far as feminism went. Their shared history of feminist organizing was matched by the "higher comfort level" they felt around the Charter. Thus, by the time the group began working on the formation of LEAF, they could draw on a "very strong collective sense" of the goal, describing their activities as "very means-oriented as opposed to results-oriented," and themselves as having "a shared sense of results."[51]

Their collective vision was reinforced during the round table discussion with this writer, given the process of collective reflection on their common history; but the closeness of their respective ideological views on the process of social change was borne out in individual interviews as well. For instance, Marilou McPhedran, commenting on her organizing efforts for the city hall educational session, remarked: "My goal for that day was to pull together a much more focused network of movers and shakers at various levels and cover off as many points of influence and to actually have in place personal commitments, knowing that people actually have these organizational resources behind their commitment."[52] Hers was a vision of women "moving change along" from within their various institutional bases. To Nancy Jackman, working through systems made sense since in her eyes women who adopted alternate tactics, such as the women of NAC who put scarves over their mouths in the House of Commons to protest women's silencing on the Meech Lake constitutional accord, only managed to marginalize their issues.[53]

There was a clear consensus that women could get what they wanted through the system by getting "the product," which was a certain way of thinking about equality, into public discourse.[54] What was needed, in their view, was Charter research "by someone other than the big boys."[55] In the same way, the participants of the round table discussion spoke of influencing the influencers with their own (female) vision of equality. It boiled down to "manipulating the system" to accommodate women's needs, using ways with which the charterwatchers as legal professionals were most at home.

It is striking how extensively this approach to social change relied on the very liberal notion of the power of reasoned argument. The founding members of LEAF shared the perception that if people were adequately informed, their interests notwithstanding, they would make the correct (i.e., just) choices. Such an assumption is premised on the notion of the free and independent self. There is, however, another contradictory element contained in this vision for social change. This is the awareness, present among most of these women, that gender does affect the outcome of social projects. Their personal and political histories (during the lobby, for example) strengthened their perception of men's and women's different interests, and their similar race and middle-class origins afforded ample opportunity to personally compare their own status to those of fathers, brothers, husbands, and male colleagues better placed in the hierarchy of power. This latter realization, in particular, can be a profoundly radicalizing experience, one enabling women to collectively name their own sex-specific reality. It is this sense of gender-based disadvantage that may have led to the resolutely apolitical position taken by most of the women active on Charter issues. Marilou McPhedran epitomized this stance when she recalled the actively hostile and rude behaviour toward the women of the Ad Hoc Committee when they lobbied for Clause 28. Considering "the reality of party structures, the reality of male-identified women, and the reality of male leaders" as she experienced them during the lobby and "the immense contempt operating in left-wing circles" toward women, McPhedran concluded: "I do my best work non-aligned."[56] Confronting the tremendous commitment expressed by endless rounds of organizing meetings, one has difficulty dismissing the efforts of these women as merely reformist and professionally comfortable activities, as some critics and historians have done when describing institutionalized feminism. The sex consciousness that emerged whenever I posed the question of the reason for their commitment recalled Foucault's words about the power of suppressed knowledge. Women, even privileged women, experience their exclusion from the status quo. This is certainly evident in the biographies of some of the women involved in charterwatching. Mary Eberts, speaking of the origin of her interest in social justice issues, remarked: "I can't ever think of a time when I had a sense that I belonged in a group that had power or was established." The experience of sex discrimination in law school was for her, as for Marilou McPhedran, intensely politicizing. For Mary Eberts, it strengthened a childhood awareness of injustice; for Marilou McPhedran, it challenged her assumption that "the system was inherently fair." Even Nancy Jackman, who was brought up in one of Toronto's wealthier families, confronted the contradiction of powerlessness stemming from gender when she fought in court for her right to remain in the United Church's ministry, and when she fought within her own family for her right to control the family's foundation.

The contradiction between class privilege and powerlessness as a woman can fuel the type of commitment evident among the charterwatchers. It can also create an unease and self-consciousness about organizing as women and in defence of women's interests. To feel, as Mary Eberts did, that as a woman you are "a member of the underclass even if you work in an environment ... which has all the trappings of 'power on Bay street'," is to be ambivalent about remaining attached to traditional institutions. The contradiction was not simply felt; it had a material base. When these women used their firms' resources for Charter activities or became publicly identified with defending women's interests, they took certain professional risks. On the other hand, as employees of such firms they enjoyed professional advantages. The feminist community, reacting to what the group has called their "yuppie image," has sometimes disparaged this form of feminist activism. Well aware that "women lawyers (professionals) are not favourites in the women's movement,"[57] the charterwatching group has defended their form of feminist activism on the basis that the project of a litigation fund required different structures and a different image from that of other feminist endeavours:

> We always knew that we would need substantial bucks. The American experience said to us that we had to structure ourselves differently from the smaller, voluntary, feminist organizations with which we had worked. We had to be an elite because we would need substantial amounts of money.[58]

The requirements of a litigation fund meant, for Marilou McPhedran, the group's funding organizer, that "some people in the organization get to stay more politically pure than others ... [the reality of funding] makes us focus

on segments of society that are a long way from basic feminist principles."
Staying within traditional institutions, such as big law firms, provided the
appropriate image and the necessary resources. For Beth Atcheson, working from within amounted to "a form of unrecognized and unknown redistribution." The contradiction of feminist activism from within the very
institutions that support women's subordination is, then, clearly one that is
openly acknowledged by the charterwatchers. In Beth Atcheson's words:
"Most of us as women fit neither into the more radical women's community
nor do we fit in these institutions.... You have got to be able to function
within that system because you're trying to make it work without betraying
the grass roots." The Women's Legal Education and Action Fund confronted this particular dilemma throughout its history.

The Birth of LEAF

In August of 1984, nine months before Section 15 of the Charter of Rights
and Freedoms came into effect, specific planning began for the birth of the
Women's Legal Education and Action Fund. The small group that met at
21 McGill, a private Toronto women's club, on August 9, 1984, began the
organizing of the fund with characteristic energy and a shared sense of
what needed to be done.[59] Besides the authors of the forthcoming *Women
and Legal Action,* the planning group for LEAF initially included Marilou
McPhedran, two well-known professional women Shelagh Day and Kathleen O'Neil, and Nancy Jackman whose importance as a potential financial
contributor to the fund would become evident over the next few months.

Events moved quickly. In September the group considered who might
form the board of LEAF, which was scheduled for birth immediately after
Section 15 came into force; by October, they had received for their use
$100,000 from the Jackman Foundation. The release of *Women and Legal
Action* that month made it clear that a litigation fund could not succeed
without a great deal of money, a requirement that made funding for LEAF
the greatest priority. High profile professional women, typically lawyers
and human rights professionals, were drawn into the organizing,[60] and
fundraising began in earnest. Kathleen O'Neil was asked to go to her organization the Federation of Women Teachers of Ontario; endorsements
were sought from the YWCA; and every conceivable network was activated
in the interests of finding the financial support for LEAF.

Kasia Seydegart was hired to plan the fundraising and suggested that the group cultivate well-known human rights advocates such as the Canadian Human Rights Commission's Gordon Fairweather (one of the three kings), and Judge Rosalie Abella who wrote the *Report of the Royal Commission on Equality in Employment* published in October 1984. By November, animated by "the dream ... to make the promise of equality contained in Section 15 a reality for all Canadian women,"[61] the group could record in the minutes their finances to date: $117,000 from the Federation of Women Teachers of Ontario ($70,000 in funds and the rest in services); an initial $50,000 from the Jackman Foundation; and $700 in smaller donations. Appeals to wealthy women and grant applications consumed the rest of 1984.

In the frenzy of organizing, LEAF women relied heavily on their traditional networks. Thus, although the minutes of January 11, 1985, contained a passing reference to the need to involve immigrant women and women of colour, and Magda Seydegart recalled pressing for community involvement,[62] the composition of both the working committee and the board remained homogeneous in character. Seventeen professional white women made up the working committee struck on December 18, 1984; eleven of them were either lawyers or human rights professionals. On April 13 and 14, 1984, when LEAF officially came into being with an elected board and an executive committee, the composition did not change.[63]

LEAF embodied the three main features recommended in *Women and Legal Action:* the establishment of a single national fund, the direct sponsorship of (preferably winnable) cases, and a complementary strategy of education and lobbying. As the epicentre of this strategy LEAF, Mary Eberts wrote, had a good chance of occupying the field of equality rights in the courtroom, but

> expertise can be applied in ways other than this case-by-case approach. Counsel and volunteers from the organization can become involved in legal writing, legal education, and continuing education of bench and bar. In this fashion, they may come to influence how decision-makers view the legal issues involved. Just as important, however, they may influence how lawyers prepare and present cases they bring forward."[64]

"Occupying the field" on equality issues in court, doing proactive litigation, influencing the influencers, were components of LEAF's vision. The criteria for selecting cases, as adopted at the founding meeting, reflected their ambitious intent. Cases taken had to concern equality rights; arise under the Charter of Rights and Freedoms or under Quebec's Charter; present strong facts; and be of importance to women. Finally, LEAF declared itself particularly interested in cases in which women were doubly disadvantaged, that is, subjected to sex discrimination as well discrimination on the basis of race, disability, etc.

A decision was made early on to begin immediately in the courtroom. On April 17, 1985, in a blaze of publicity, LEAF announced its first two cases – one concerned the right of married women to keep their own names, and the other attacked the requirement that welfare recipients, the majority of whom are women, live as single persons in order to qualify for assistance. Beth Symes described the day:

> [Counsel] Eloise Spitzer's name change case involved the Yukon, a Francophone [Suzanne Bertrand, a French Canadian living in the Yukon who wished to retain her maiden name because it reflected her French-Canadian ancestry] and a blatant case we could win. The second case, the spouse-in-the-house case, was chosen [because] it was for disadvantaged women and because it was a symbol of the state oppressiveness [toward] women. April 17 was a wonderful spectacle on the hill. We raised $20,000 that day in Ottawa and $25,000 in Toronto.[65]

It was an auspicious beginning, full of hope and confidence and undeterred by the enormity of the task at hand.

LEAF's founders were marked by a consistency of vision that few women's organizations can boast. Best summed up by their own self-description, "we don't argue about things that are system-driven,"[66] their approach was undeniably one born out of a profound belief that the system, in particular the legal system, can accommodate women's needs. Yet, the intense commitment that fuelled this vision came out of an awareness of women's subordinate status, and men's active efforts to protect their dominance. This personally and politically experienced contradiction was to play itself out over the next three years in a political climate in which men's use of the Charter destroyed any plan to have a proactive approach. LEAF found itself reacting, as women before them had done in court, to cases brought by men that threatened the few legal gains women already possessed. Additionally, the equality vision, an equality of rights that had seemed so deceptively simple and straightforward, would raise issues both in and out of the courtroom; issues that would highlight the difference gender makes in our society.

Equality of Results

Equality of results was clearly the prevailing rhetoric of the 1980s. Federal government reports, while they did little to concretely achieve it, did not quarrel with its major premises: that inequality was a group phenomenon, that white men could no longer be the norm against which everyone was measured, and that equality meant the recognition of both biological and social differences. Even the courts had begun to accept some of these perceptions. In the *O'Malley* case, involving the demotion of a woman whose newly-acquired religious beliefs prevented her from working on Saturdays, The Honourable Mr Justice McIntyre ruled that "it is the result or the effect of the action complained of which is significant. If it does, in fact, cause discrimination, if its effect is to impose on one person or group of persons obligations, penalties or restrictive conditions not imposed on other members of the community, then it is discriminatory."[67] Thus when Lynn Smith declared, in an article first presented at the symposium on equality rights, that equality is measured by whether it means "equal results for women in light of their reality, as it does for men in light of their reality,"[68] she was expressing a results-oriented view of equality advanced by some members of the judiciary, the legal profession, human rights professionals, women's groups, and groups representing Native people, disabled people, and visible minorities.

When the focus shifts from abstract equality to equality as measured in the pay and opportunities enjoyed by various groups, when we speak of "equality-seekers" rather than target groups,[69] and when we insist that the norm has to shift away from white men,[70] how much have we escaped the perils of liberal rights discourse? To begin with, we are still implicitly ordering our perception according to the notion of comparison. Equality in its liberal roots stresses the equal distribution of resources to which we are entitled on the basis of our common humanity as rational beings. The norm may shift, and we may recognize that other groups are entitled to their fair share, but the problems of evaluating competing equality claims, now between groups, persist. Justice is still our preoccupation and it precludes other, perhaps more valuable goals. As one LEAF activist reflected,

> LEAF's basic premise is that equality with men is the desirable objective (plus of course consideration for biological differences such as maternity). This is what is limiting – [it] doesn't allow for wider policy innovations such as less workaholism, lifelong learning, shifting values to peace, clean environments, except indirectly. [71]

Jill Vickers has made the same point as well, noting that equality-seekers seldom trouble to envision what equality would actually be like. [72] Specifically, this framework inhibits any thinking about the nature of community and its difference from other communities, *except in terms of how much of society's resources each possesses.*

Significantly, however, the new insistence on looking at equality through the lens of inequality led women to the point of examining and communicating to men the nature of their lived oppression. For LEAF, from 1985 onward, this process happened in a court of law and within the context of confrontation.

CHAPTER TWO

LEAF LITIGATION
IN CONTEXT

L ITIGATION AS feminist activity embodies an obvious contradiction: it is in essence the telling of women's stories in a language and a setting structured to deny the relevance of women's experiences. Those who do the telling, the men and women lawyers, the "experts" and the women whose lives are thus exposed, live this contradiction often in a painful way. For the women of LEAF, particularly those who are closely involved in LEAF's courtroom activities and who also practice law for a living, the experience of being feminist in the legal world, of functioning effectively as lawyers without betraying grass-roots women's communities has been likened to schizophrenia,[1] a disease characterized by the unnatural separation of thought and emotion.

LEAF's organizational profile illustrates the tensions that result and the dilemmas LEAF confronts as a simultaneously legal and feminist organization. As well, all the cases it supports require a delicate balancing of challenge without threat. LEAF asks the court to examine its own rules critically, yet at the same time it must operate within those rules or risk losing the chance to be heard; it asks a predominantly male bench to hear evidence about and to relate to facets of the experience of being female in a patriarchal society; and it pleads for equality while noting that the equality standard itself is a trap for women.

51

An Organizational Profile

When the Women's Legal Education and Action Fund officially came into being on April 17, 1985, its founders intended its structure to replicate the best features of American litigation funds and to avoid their worst short-comings. Impressed by the record of the American organization the National Association for the Advancement of Colored People (NAACP), in particular their strategy of pursuing incremental gains in specific areas, LEAF's founders concluded that Canadian women could best secure their legal rights in a similar way. In American terminology, the NAACP approach was to "occupy" a particular area of law and become known as the expert litigators in that field, and by selecting winnable issues and controlling the development of case law judges could be asked to take small steps at any one time. Such a long-term strategy of staged litigation requires considerable funding, preferably from a broad, non-governmental base. The intention is for the litigating organization to act as the sponsor of a party to the case, financially a more onerous role than that of intervenor where an organization acts as a "friend of the court" and limits its participation to offering a written and oral opinion on how the case affects the interests it promotes.[2] In the United States, the vision of a proactive legal fund usually involves lobbying and public education, activities that mandate a close relationship with feminist communities.

LEAF's founders intended to pursue a proactive strategy involving the building of test cases. Accordingly, they developed five criteria for case selection, and, following Karen O'Connor's recommendations in her book on American women's legal organizations, they erected a structure to complement the strategy of seeking out important cases nationally, researching them, and having the financial resources to shepherd cases through the lengthy and costly court process. O'Connor also emphasized the importance of strong national headquarters and highly-skilled legal volunteers, the value of publicity both for funders and for credibility in the legal community, the value of local affiliates in keeping the organization in touch with its constituency, and the importance of both legal and public education.[3] Conspicuously absent was any mechanism for ensuring the legal fund's accountability to feminist communities.

LEAF's structure acknowledged the importance of the factors O'Connor outlined. Its board of directors included a national chair and vice-chair, a national legal committee made up of representatives from across the country, finance and fundraising chairs, a chair of public education and research, and local affiliates on the prairies, in the Yukon, and on the west and east coasts.

Two salient features of LEAF, as a women's organization and as one involved primarily in legal activities that require large sums of money, bear closer examination for they reveal the source of contradictions and tensions that permeated the organization and its activities in court. Legal work is highly specialized work and it is typically performed under considerable time constraints. These two factors, as well as the corporate environment in which much legal work is done, and indeed the basic assumptions of legal discourse that have to do with the search for a rational objective truth that is provable through precedent, all contribute to a style of work that is normally hierarchical and closed. As Mary Eberts put it, the "image of the great senior counsel who has all his minions doing his work for him is really a very familiar archetype."[4] The image, as Eberts pointed out, is compatible with the traditional role of the legal advocate as being the one individual responsible for presenting the case in court. In this format, it is difficult to allow for the consultation and community so necessary when various voices are to be heard. The problem of legal narrowing and control by one or two individuals is further exacerbated when all of the participants of the legal team typically share the same class and race origins and, as legal professionals, have all been schooled in the assumptions and practices of liberal legalism.

LEAF's first litigation report recognized that "selecting the right test cases for litigation involves a careful process of winnowing, investigation and research."[5] Typically (and LEAF, as I show below, has not been typical in this respect), someone brings a possible test case or, more commonly, a legal problem women have experienced to the organization's attention. The staff then proceeds to research the issue involved, meeting with a variety of legal consultants before it reaches the legal committee for consideration. Unless one or more of the consultants contacted have a strong community orientation, and unless there are sufficient time and resources to seek consultation further afield, only the legal aspects of the issue are considered. For LEAF, then, as a feminist organization seeking to protect and improve women's legal rights essentially through the telling of women's stories in court, the first challenge is to accommodate a variety of women's voices to a process that fundamentally negates consultation and difference.

Attracting the large sums of money that litigation requires also places a women's legal defence fund under greater than usual pressure to respond to funders' desires.[6] LEAF's founders knew from the beginning that a broad funding base was desirable,[7] but in actively pursuing it those involved in funding gained a keen appreciation of the compromises in image that would be required. To Marilou McPhedran, the group's chief fundraiser at several points in its history, fundraising meant "breaking into those echelons where feminists have never been very comfortable"[8] and presenting an appropriate image for corporate and government funders that spoke of LEAF women's credibility as members of the legal, not the feminist, community. To another LEAF founder, Beth Atcheson, LEAF had to appear to be an elite corps because this was the only way to garner sufficient financial support from those most able to give it.[9] This left LEAF, however, in the position of being attractive to its funders but alienated from the feminist communities it served and needed. When LEAF hosted a $100-a-plate dinner, it raised funds from the middle and upper classes but strengthened its image as an organization with few ties to women in the community. Moreover, as the beneficiaries of relatively large government grants, LEAF was vulnerable to the rancour of some segments of the community who felt that litigation activities attracted more governmental support than grass-roots activities – rape crisis centres, for example.

Perhaps because of who in Canadian society are legally trained and the necessity of attracting large sums of money (and therefore being "credible" to potential corporate and government funders), LEAF's founders and its main activists, as we have seen, were a remarkably homogeneous group[10] who for the most part chose to remain professionally anchored in the corporate legal world. LEAF women themselves have noted that one way of coming to terms with the contradiction of a feminist challenge from within the corporate world is to capitalize on this insider status. LEAF certainly reflected this approach: it used the resources of large law firms, the status of well-known litigators, and its own credibility as a legal organization with elite connections (when lobbying governments, for example) to contribute to its success. In both its internal and external activities, however, an organization that operates in this fashion runs the risk of losing the self-critical edge that comes with a diversity of races, classes, and occupations. It might also be argued, as Andrea Nye has argued of women who must work within the language of patriarchal discourse, that "respectability is inevitably self-defeating" because challenge is unlikely to be sustained from within.[11] Those who felt at odds with the style and approach of LEAF women found it hard to participate. Indeed, for many would-be supporters of LEAF it was LEAF's image as an "intellectual, trail-blazing organization" with a stellar legal cast that was attractive,[12] while others mentioned their early sense of discomfort with the organization's "corporatist-feminist"[13] approach and the priority litigation had, at least in the first two years of LEAF's operation, over the building of a strong community base.

Commenting on LEAF's tendency in its first two years to concentrate on the goals rather than the process of its particular feminist activity, Mary Eberts recalled, by way of explanation, the sense of urgency that characterized the early LEAF, that is the feeling that if LEAF were not off and running toward the goal of occupying the field of equality litigation there would not be another chance to influence the course of jurisprudence: "I question whether a more traditional process-oriented women's group would have been able to take LEAF where it went in its first two years, whereas now, I think it can change its methods."[14] LEAF's style of operation and its homogeneity may well have aided its early objectives, if at the cost of its image among other feminists, but these attributes also contributed to limiting the kind of community contact that is vital to selecting and researching appropriate issues for litigation. Two examples illustrate this effect and also serve to illustrate LEAF's evolution into an organization better able to accommodate and learn from different voices.

In what was to become a trend of disturbing significance, men began to use the Charter soon after its promulgation to protest against the few protections women enjoyed in law. In one of these cases, *Seaboyer/Gayme*,[15] two men accused of rape protested that their right to a fair trial as guaranteed in the Charter was infringed upon because of provisions in the Criminal Code that prohibited using as evidence a victim's previous sexual history (except in three specific instances). LEAF applied for and was granted intervenor status whereupon it had thirty days to submit its legal argument concerning why these "rape shield" provisions should continue to stand. In what was intended to be a strategic move, LEAF hired a well-known male criminal lawyer who prepared a somewhat scant brief for the court; it included some examples of possible infringements on the right to a fair trial that might result from the rape shield provisions of the Criminal Code. Further, the approach taken was a rather conservative one where no mention was made of the relationship between these provisions in the Code and women's right to equality under Section 15 of the Charter.[16] A group of feminists working on the possibility of civil remedies for women harmed by pornography were highly critical of the LEAF brief, pointing out the lack of equality arguments and noting particularly the ill-advised examples that conceded there may be times when a woman's previous sexual history may be relevant to a determination of whether or not she was raped.[17]

For LEAF, the *Seaboyer/ Gayme* case was its first reminder of the perils of not seeking consultation within the wider feminist community. To its credit, the organization then responded constructively to criticism and developed a process of "workshopping" cases with working groups of feminists who had specific expertise on the issues under consideration. Indeed, the working group formed to discuss what had gone wrong in *Seaboyer/ Gayme* remained active for subsequent cases, and workshopping has continued to be the approach taken, the cost of such consultation notwithstanding.[18] According to Mary Eberts, a working group is formed for cases where there is enough lead time, consisting of a member of the national legal committee and/or LEAF's executive director, volunteer lawyers, and representatives from the local LEAF chapter. Each working group develops its own links with the women's community. As the report on the second year of LEAF litigation commented: "Developing case strategy requires a sure vision about the meaning of equality and how that theory should be made concrete in this particular instance, a vision that cannot be arrived at in isolation."[19]

In its dealings with the visible minority women's community of Toronto, at least initially, workshopping did not save LEAF from the kind of misunderstandings and friction that develop when an all white, predominantly middle-class organization begins working on issues concerning immigrant and visible minority women. Early in 1986, LEAF worked with the Centre for Spanish Speaking Peoples and prepared a challenge to the federal language training policies that deny language training to women entering Canada as sponsored immigrants. In the ensuing consultations, LEAF found that it had stumbled into a controversy within the immigrant women's community over which groups and individual women had the right to speak on behalf of that community. In a memo she submitted to the National Organization of Immigrant and Visible Minority Women of Canada, Carmencita Hernandez questioned LEAF's "ability and sensitivity to represent the interests and perspectives of immigrant and visible minority women whose mother tongue is neither English nor French."[20] The specific grievances against LEAF were complicated, involving LEAF's unawareness of the controversy surrounding a colloquium held in Toronto on the issue of federal language training. The colloquium was organized and supported by representatives of immigrant women's groups with whom LEAF had consulted and boycotted by other individuals and groups from various visible minority women's communities. What did become clear from the ensuing tensions, however, was LEAF's lack of knowledge of this important segment of the women's community. In subsequent discussions of the issue, LEAF women's responses have ranged from anger and hostility at the visible minority community for being so quick to condemn[21] to a careful acknowledgement that "this is one example of an issue where the community that's involved regards it as probably more important to have a process to bring the case under its own control than it does to win the case."[22]

While it remains to be seen whether or not LEAF will recognize and accommodate the political importance of process over legal goals and build links with communities whose perspectives are not represented in its ranks, it is clear that its homogeneity and overwhelming focus on the legal aspects of issues hamper existing relations between it and different feminist communities. Despite its increased involvement in a broad range of issues affecting women at the community level, LEAF's legal and lobbying activities continue to ensure a certain insularity from other women's communities. For example, in 1987 it devoted a considerable amount of attention to the revised constitutional agreements, known as the Meech Lake Accord. In contrast to the lobbying around Sections 15 and 28 five years earlier, LEAF encountered substantial state resistance to its position that the Accord jeopardized the hard-won equality guarantees of the Charter.

While the Accord challenged all that LEAF stood for, it hardly touched the concerns of local women's groups – an indication of the continuing need to build bridges between the "institutionalized" feminist sector and other groups in the community. [23]

LEAF's elitist image was reinforced when one of its founders, with the aid of Mary Eberts, personally fought (and won) her case for the right of self-employed women to deduct child care expenses from their income tax. This approach to the child care problem was explicitly rejected by the Canadian Day Care Advocacy Association as being beneficial to middle- and upper-class women at the expense of others. LEAF, by association, came under fire for being isolationist. [24] The fact that the case was taken up on the personal initiative of Beth Symes and her lawyer Mary Eberts, and not under the auspices of LEAF, did little to dispel suspicion.

When we turn to the examination of LEAF litigation, it is with the question in mind of LEAF's activities within the context of the women's movement. To what extent have the issues LEAF has taken up, and the manner in which it has done so, challenged the social order that oppresses women and minorities, and what has been the impact of this challenge? Richard Kluger, commenting on the NAACP's litigation activities, noted that "lawsuits are proceedings too technical and lengthy to form the basis for a mass movement, though they set that movement in motion." [25] More optimistically, Elizabeth Schneider wrote that rights discourse in the courts can be used to express "the politics, vision, and demands of a social movement, and to assist in the political self-definition of that movement." [26] In LEAF's case, its ability to do just this effectively was possibly constrained by the nature of legal games and by LEAF's homogeneity; but, it is really only in its litigation activities that one can properly explore whether or not feminism applied to law survives intact as a political activity that improves the lives of women. Furthermore, in asking these kinds of questions, it will be important to keep in mind the long-term process of securing equality through the courts and the complex uneven way in which law affects the status of women.

The Judicial Climate in the 1980s

Litigating on behalf of women in a Canadian court was different in certain significant respects from that activity in the UnitedStates during the early 1980s. The social, political, and judicial climate in Canada appeared to offer certain advantages or cracks in the system that could work to the advantage of Canadian women, at least for the moment. Of course, there were also important barriers to successful litigation, notably, anti-feminist reaction spawned in the wake of women visibly promoting their rights. And LEAF laboured under constraints of its own, for instance the difficulty of funding and the growth in its case load.

American women oriented their litigation activities in the late 1970s toward winning acceptance of the principle that sex discrimination deserved as serious judicial scrutiny as did race discrimination. They, therefore, focused on those instances of sex discrimination which involved "facial" discrimination, that is, they focused on cases in which it was obvious that women were differentially treated because of their biological characteristics – pregnancy, for example. Their litigation efforts failed, however, leaving them with the ongoing struggle of showing how women as a group are adversely affected by certain practices.

In 1980 Margaret Berger, reporting on the progress of women's litigation funds in the United States, noted that when it came to women American courts had not accepted the concept of disparate impact. Also known as adverse impact, disparate impact was a policy or a practice that could unintentionally restrict or disfavour the members of a particular group. Ironically, the path-breaking case involving the concept of unintentional adverse impact as it applied to race discrimination won judicial approval as early as 1971.[27] Had American women won the judicial acceptance of the notion of adverse impact as it applied to them, they could have argued that routine practices, such as insurance schemes that treated pregnant workers differently from other workers, discriminated against women as a group even though no individual intent to discriminate against specific pregnant women could be traced. The conservative climate ushered in by Ronald Reagan, in which American women saw the defeat of the Equal Rights Amendment to their constitution, which might have strengthened the judicial commitment to taking sex discrimination seriously, did little to alleviate this state of affairs.

In contrast, Canadian women fought for and won Charter provisions that acknowledged the need to address substantive inequality sustained by unintentional practices adversely affecting them. Section 15 explicitly stated that Canadians were not to be discriminated against on the basis of race and sex, among other characteristics, and that all Canadians enjoyed equal benefit and protection of the law – phrases meant to protect disadvantaged groups from the unintended harm of routine or systemic practices. Indeed, by 1985 when LEAF began to litigate, the concept of adverse impact had won important judicial acceptance in Canada. For example, in a much quoted decision on the *Big M* case over the legitimacy of laws banning Sunday shopping, the court declared unequivocally that the "meaning of a right or freedom guaranteed by the Charter was to be ascertained by an analysis of the *purpose* of such a guarantee; it was to be understood, in other words, in the light of the interests it was meant to protect."[28] The court then went on to make clear that paying heed to the interests involved, that is to the impact of a practice on particular groups, meant that "the interests of true equality may well require differentiation in treatment."[29] Although Sunday shopping laws had little to do with women's rights *per se* (except women were among those workers and consumers affected), Canadian women arguing for recognition of their special needs and maintaining that the Charter signified the importance of sex equality were much heartened by this decision because of the pronouncements it contained on equality and on the meaning of rights in the Charter. If laws or practices had to take into account their impact on specific groups, then women could argue that policies or practices that disadvantaged them were illegal, regardless of the intent of those who formulated them. Further, they could argue for policies or practices that met their needs even if this meant that women were treated differently than men.

Decisions on cases originating in Human Rights Commissions in 1985 also indicated consistent support for the concept of adverse impact. For example, in a case involving religious freedom, *O'Malley v. Simpsons Sears,* the court held that no intent was necessary to prove that a practice had discriminatory impact.[30] In the celebrated case of *Action Travail des*

Femmes, where the Canadian National Railway was found guilty of block-ing the hiring of women, the court, noting the findings of disadvantage suf-fered by women and minorities as documented in the *Report of the Royal Commission on Equality in Employment,* again ruled that what counted was the impact rather than the intent of discriminatory practices. If these early human rights decisions gave women litigating for their rights some hope, some early Charter decisions sustained their optimism. In *R. v. Oakes,* the Supreme Court of Canada reinforced the importance of equality guaran-tees in the Charter. The court supported the view that once an infringe-ment of a right has been found to have occurred the onus then shifts to the party denying the right to prove under Section 1 of the Charter that the limitation is reasonable and demonstrably justified.[31] Proof under this sec-tion had to be stringent and paying due heed to the values of the Charter. In *Edwards Books v. R.* the court issued a warning that the Charter not be used to benefit those already advantaged or to take rights away from the disad-vantaged.[32] Thus, when LEAF went to court with its first cases in 1985, it did so with reasonable optimism.

Damage Control

While the progress made in winning acceptance of the principle of adverse impact was heartening, LEAF had no sooner begun its litigation activities when it became clear that, the favourable judicial climate of the 1980s not-withstanding, it would not be able to maintain the type of control over equality litigation it had originally anticipated. More was at stake than judicial recognition of unintentional discrimination. As Beth Symes rue-fully reflected at the round table discussion in 1988, in which LEAF's foun-ders discussed their achievements and common history:

> If you're going to build law with respect to equality, you want to build it your way. So therefore, you flood the courts with your cases and your issues in the order in which you want the court to hear them. We have not occupied the field. Men have. We have been involved in damage control ... men have been popping up all over Canada in various courts challenging things that we as women fought to get, such as maternity benefits, such as the rape shield provisions. Resources have gone into these interventions.[33]

LEAF's careful building of feminist jurisprudence based on precedent and their planning the court's progress toward acceptance of key concepts fell by the wayside when proactive quickly turned to reactive and LEAF found itself acting as a third party, as an intervenor in cases brought by men. They were thereby forced to abandon their agenda and respond to one set by men's claims for equality. The intervention process poses two major constraints: first, it involves extreme time pressures (only thirty days remain from the time an appeal is filed to the time an intervenor must file its request for intervention); once granted the status to intervene, an intervenor then has a further thirty days from the time the last party's factum (written argument) is filed to file her own. Second, as one American legal advocate has observed, the lawyer representing the (male) party bringing the case to court has a considerable advantage in characterizing the issue.[34] Canadian intervenors are required to speak to the specific interests they claim to defend and are seldom empowered to bring evidence, cross-examine, or expand upon the issue in any way. LEAF women entered the legal fray under these constraints, factors that influenced their success more than the benefits of an otherwise favourable judicial climate.

Overview of LEAF *Cases*

In its first three years of litigation, LEAF opened over three hundred files. Of these, it adopted sixty-four cases for consideration by the legal committee, pursuing over thirty in some detail. Its caseload far exceeded capacity, and in 1989 LEAF had to limit its acceptance of intake calls to one day of the week.[35] While there were cases where LEAF took a proactive approach, initiating court action and seeking to build on acceptance of such concepts as adverse impact (and these naturally had a longer gestation time than others), most of its cases to date were those in which LEAF acted as an intervenor, defending women's interests in cases brought by men. Thus, at the board's annual meeting in June of 1986, decisions were made to concentrate on proactive work in the two major areas of employment law and income assistance for low-income women (areas where routine policies or practices had an adverse impact on certain groups of women), and to establish a strategy to cope with the epidemic of cases brought by men. As the board concluded, "the strong Charter attacks brought by men against legislative protection for victims of sexual assault were thought to require an appropriate response."[36] An overview of LEAF's litigation activities reveals the complex and myriad ways in which law, as legislation or as bureaucratic regulation, reinforces the inequality of women. In each one of its cases, ranging from the symbolic to the immediately relevant, LEAF confronted a deeply entrenched patriarchy, a system that must have seemed at times like Hercules' nine-headed hydra. Each time one of its heads was cut off, two more immediately sprung up in its place. But if patriarchy appeared invincible, its interconnectedness meant that a challenge in one area often had ripple effects in another and it is this vulnerability that LEAF women profitably exploited.

LEAF's first court case on April 17, 1985, was a challenge to the Vital Statistics Act (of various provinces) that required children to carry the surnames of their fathers. Although it carried a symbolic value that was immediately apparent, its practical implications and urgency must have eluded many women. Few social customs illustrate so clearly the concept of men's ownership of women and children and, as Carol Smart points out, a challenge in this area suggests women's independence in a graphic and threatening way.[37] LEAF, aware that the principle of equality in this area (i.e., that both parents had the right to pass on their surnames) had been accepted by provincial governments but not acted upon in practice, intended by this and subsequent challenges to erect the first block of winnable cases and clearly establish equality principles. The name cases LEAF defended offered it an opportunity to state unequivocally that the "custom of naming of children exclusively after the father is the product of a patriarchal society where children were identified through their fathers, just as wives were identified through their husbands," a position LEAF considered to be the first step in judicial education on "the social and cultural history of a particular instance of oppression."[38] Most of the name cases were settled out of court.[39]

From name changes, LEAF moved on to defend twelve-year-old Justine Blainey's right to play hockey on a boys' team. Although she qualified, Blainey was prohibited from joining by a regulation of the Ontario Hockey Association. Ironically, the regulation, protected by a section of the Ontario Human Rights Code exempting amateur sports associations from prosecution because of membership discrimination on the basis of sex, was originally intended to protect the single-sex sports organizations that women and girls needed to foster their potential. The Ontario Hockey Association argued that the regulation was needed to prevent the integration of women's hockey; Justine Blainey's special needs would, in this instance, have to be superseded in favour of women's needs in general.

LEAF was thus confronted with arguing for an individual girl's right to play on a boys' hockey team as well as for the right of girls (and women) as a group to have separate teams. The case's attraction lay in the opposing side's argument that "sex equality must in every instance be perfectly symmetrical";[40] a position that, if accepted, would make it difficult to respond to women's needs across a variety of situations. As well, the judge hearing the initial application displayed remarkable confusion between what might be justified under Section 15(2) of the Charter as an affirmative action measure and what might be ruled sex discrimination under Section 15(1) promoting equality in the administration and the substance of the law. In this sense, the case possessed an importance that went beyond the equality issues affecting Justine Blainey. In LEAF's view, a favourable decision in Blainey "would be of enormous benefit" to the case then before the courts involving a challenge to the exclusively female membership base of the Federation of Women Teachers.[41] (In fact, the issue of women's right to form single-sex organizations whenever their equality interests would be better served to do so did crop up again in 1988 when a local men's group challenged their exclusion from a women's self-defense course.)[42]

However, the Ontario Court of Appeal ruled that the Blainey case was outside the ambit of the Charter because it concerned a regulation of the Ontario Hockey Association and not a law made by Parliament – a significant difference since the constitution can only be used to challenge state action – and found the discrimination against Justine Blainey to be embedded in the Human Rights Code itself. Eventually, Justine Blainey's rights were assessed by a one-man board of inquiry of the Ontario Human Rights Commission, and on January 14, 1988, it decided that she could play on a boys' team.[43]

From its inception, LEAF recognized that women's status was often determined not by the letter of the law itself but by the network of bureaucratic rules and regulations in their day-to-day application. One of its first proactive cases epitomized the law's far reaches into women's lives. In

Ontario, sole-support mothers (and recently, fathers) are entitled to eco-nomic support on the condition that they live as single persons. Although framed in gender-neutral terms (i.e., reference to spousal relationships), this policy is based on the assumption that women in intimate relationships with men were usually economically supported by those men. To challenge these spouse-in-the-house or, more accurately, man-in-the-house regula-tions (the majority of sole-support claimants are heterosexual women), LEAF accepted the cases of Shiela Beaudette and Brenda Horvath, who were denied family benefits (without appeal) because of a finding that they sustained friendships with men in quasi-spousal capacities. In Beaudette's case, a male friend helped her get credit and on one occasion took her chil-dren out to a restaurant – activities which were thought to be typical of a spouse. In Horvath's case, a male friend with whom she was not living helped her get a lease on an apartment. Since a government committee was in the process of investigating welfare policies, it was in the forum of a com-mittee rather than the courtroom that LEAF expressed its concerns. [44]

The assumptions underlying the spouse-in-the-house regulations, that women could expect to be economically supported by men, prevailed in bureaucratic regulations elsewhere. LEAF challenged Ontario's farm assis-tance programs (providing assistance to first-time farmers) that prohibited the spouses of farmers from applying; it took up the case of a Manitoba housewife who found that the province's public insurance scheme paid housewives lower disability benefits than it paid to others; and it entered into negotiations with the federal government over the differential pen-sions it paid to men and women. In all of these cases, LEAF's negotiations with the bureaucracy were underscored by the potential for court action.

LEAF's proactive efforts required this blend of bureaucratic and legal challenge in the spouse-in-the-house case, and in more recent initiatives such as challenges to labour laws restricting the rights of domestic workers, to federal language training policies denying training to sponsored immi-grants, and to the policies and practices of the Prison for Women (known as P4W). In applying their feminism to law in these areas, LEAF women were in fact exposing how a variety of institutions operated on a day-to-day basis to entrench women's inequality. On an individual case basis, as I show below, this meant an endless round of negotiations over what is fair and what is politically feasible in the specific instance. Taken as a whole, however, these challenges begin to look much more like a frontal attack on the routines of inequality.

Men's use of the Charter and the cases they brought forward took LEAF, as intervenor, into unfamiliar territory. These cases fell into two categories: cases where an opportunity presented itself to secure a gain for women or where what was sought was an extension of a right to both men and women, and cases where the issue was the loss of rights women already possess in law. In the first group, cases where women might make inroads into Charter jurisprudence, LEAF had an opportunity to be a great deal more creative in the application of feminism to law. For instance, in recognition of its legitimacy as an organization able to speak on the interests of women, LEAF was granted intervenor status, including leave to call witnesses, cross-examine, and make argument in Shalom Schachter's challenge of unemployment insurance regulations which then provided for parental leave for adoptive fathers and not for natural fathers. Fearing that the case would simply result in the cutting back of the fifteen weeks leave currently granted to the mother, if the leave were to be shared between both parents, LEAF acted to ensure that the remedy sought by Mr Schachter did not have an indirect negative impact on the mother's leave. It thus argued that the leave provisions be extended to include leave for mothers and natural and adoptive fathers. LEAF asked in this instance that the court "read up" legislation by extending the current leave provisions, an initiative courts usually referred to the legislature.

LEAF acted as intervenor in the similar case of *Shewchuk v. Ricard* where the alleged father of a child was being sued for support by the child's mother. In his defence, the father argued that since the British Columbia Child Support and Paternity Act entitled a mother, and not a father, to sue for maintenance, his right to equality under Section 15 of the Charter was being denied. LEAF intervened and argued that the legislation should include both fathers and mothers, again fearing that if the man's claim were honoured, mothers would lose their right to sue for support.

In the case brought by Mark David Andrews challenging the regulation of the Law Society of British Columbia requiring that lawyers be Canadian citizens, LEAF gained an opportunity to address in court the legal rule of similarly situated and its adverse impact on women. The similarly situated rule was used to justify the Law Society's exclusion of non-citizens in the first court decision. As the Law Society argued, non-citizens were not similarly situated, that is, they were not in the same position as citizens; they were, in the society's view, less acquaintanted with Canadian customs. Hence, it was justifiable to treat non-citizens differently from citizens by requiring them to become citizens before practising law.[45] Women, of course, had often borne the consequences of exclusion on the basis of their different situations, as I have discussed in chapter two.

While the opportunity existed in the *Schachter, Shewchuk,* and *Andrews* cases to secure additional rights for both men and women, as in most other cases, there was also the very real possibility that women would lose existing rights. Two cases in this group, where such a threat was particularly imminent, were the ones involving violence against women. The first of these, *Seaboyer/Gayme* discussed above, concerned two alleged rapists who challenged the rape shield provisions of the Criminal Code. The second, *Canadian Newspapers,* involved a newspaper's objection to the section of the Criminal Code that prevents a rape victim's name and identity from being published against her will. This provision is intended to encourage victims to report crimes of rape and protect them from public humiliation. The Canadian Newspapers Company considered this restriction in violation of its right to free speech. LEAF sought the opportunity to defend the provision on the basis that sex assault is a sex equality issue requiring special measures given the conditions under which most women live.

Increasingly LEAF found itself addressing issues of violence against women in a proactive way. For instance, it took up the case of a rape victim who wished to argue that because the police knew the routines of a habitual rapist in her area and failed to adequately warn and protect women, they exposed her to the threat of rape and thereby infringed upon her right to security of the person. The so-called balcony rapist case took LEAF into an area where it had to argue for women's positive right to live free of violence, an argument that poses a considerable challenge to the myth that men and women are equally situated in society. In the same way, LEAF undertook the defence of incest survivors who are prohibited by the statute of limitations from suing their abusers. Novel in the initiative they expressed, these cases profited from the equality theory developed in LEAF's sexual assault cases.[46] LEAF also took up sexual harassment cases and raised the legal issues that would give due recognition to the harm that women suffer in this area. Thus, it has argued that sexual harassment is a compensative work injury and in the case of *Jansen and Govereau v. Platy* that sexual harassment is a major impediment to women's employment equality.

Violence to their person was also the theme in LEAF cases involving women's right to control of their own bodies. In the British Columbia case of *Baby R.*, LEAF intervened to protest the court's decision that the apprehension of a foetus, thereby enabling the child welfare authorities to force a woman in labour to undergo a Caesarean section, was a legal seizure. LEAF's concern here, and in the case brought by anti-abortion crusader Joe Borowski, was the precedent that foetal rights exist, and that they exist at the expense of the mother's rights. Again, an outwardly legal argument over the balancing of rights can have far-reaching implications for women, opening the door to control of their person in the interests of the foetus. In these cases, LEAF had to counteract the major assumption of liberal legalism that individuals exist autonomously. In this world view, foetuses are seen as independent of the maternal body upon which they depend, and their very real interrelationship is a context considered tangential to the issues at hand. Similarly in cases where women are discriminated against on the basis of pregnancy, LEAF must again plead for context, arguing a decade after the *Bliss* decision that pregnancy is a sex characteristic and not a condition that is always voluntarily assumed.

What patterns can one discern from the very wide net cast by LEAF? Clearly women's engagement with the law was as women and not as citizens. That is to say, women have gone to court to argue for control of their bodies, their sexuality, their dual role as citizens and as wives and mothers, and for the right to live free of violence. LEAF's litigation on behalf of women has been exposing the soft underbelly of patriarchy. The myths of equality and individual freedom are powerful ones in our society; however, to talk about what happens to women on a daily basis – in sport, in welfare, in institutions and bureaucracies, in the home, on the streets, and on the job – is to introduce a complex reality that negates such ideals. It is to clash head on with patriarchy and the liberal discourse on which it feeds. The challenge is softened when the focus is on a single case, and it is here that LEAF can hope to have an impact.

The Art of Litigating on Behalf of Women

The application of feminism to law, that is litigation on behalf of women, has been described by Lynn Smith, one of LEAF's volunteer litigators, as "very much of an art rather than a science."[47] In Mary Eberts' view, "craft as well as theory has a place in influencing the development of jurisprudence under the Charter.[48] Possibly lawyers litigating on other issues in Charter jurisprudence would share the views of LEAF women on the nature of litigation, although to do so implicitly challenges the myths of law's rationality and neutrality and its reliance on empirical facts and precedent. What then might distinguish a feminist use of the courts from any other? How is telling women's stories in court a different process from the telling of other kinds of stories?

For Mary Eberts,[49] who acknowledged that during its first three years she played the role of "chief conspirator" on LEAF's legal team, legal advocacy on behalf of women was a process that revolved around bringing details about women's lives and the female way of thinking to the attention of a male or "male-stream" judiciary. The premise of this process was the view that "women perceive reality differently because women have always been an underclass and always see power relations differently from men." The task by her own admission is an exceedingly difficult one since by and large evidence about the reality of women's lives is regarded by the court as "creating a type of problem that is unmanageable by judicial standards." Seldom empirically validated, usually anecdotal, and telling of a reality of group oppression that stands in contravention of the precepts of legal liberalism, women's accounts of their daily lives have indeed been inadmissible in court. Asking a court to pay attention to daily life and to the oppression that forms the basis of women's experience requires new techniques in the legal game of judicial management.

One quintessential liberal approach is judicial education, informing judges through the publication of legal articles and conferences. Another more immediate tactic, and one that is common to litigation on the whole, is to assemble the "facts" of the case, the "decision-making matrix," in such a way that the judge is given little room to rely on his own (probably) stereotypical ideas of women and must rely instead on the evidence that is put before him. That evidence indirectly asks him to confront his stereo-types, but because it is presented as a problem related only to the particular issue under consideration, a strictly legal rather than an abstract philo-sophical problem, litigators like Mary Eberts hope that it is an entry into challenging "the basic mind-set" with which judges think. Challenge at this level is of course essential since judges bring their race, sex, and class-derived "intellectual baggage" to court.

Using the facts of a specific case to challenge prevailing ideas about women's reality does resemble, outwardly at least, litigating in other con-texts. Lawyers do seek to appeal to the underlying assumptions of judges. But judges' ideas about women, in contrast to their ideas about other sub-jects, although they might both be governed by the rules of a discourse that emphasize the rational and separates the public from the private, evoke an altogether unique response. Postmodernists remind us that all that scien-tific discourse would suppress is also what we think of as the feminine, the world of emotion, community, and the ties that bind us to each other. Once we begin to think of individuals as part of their communities, the balancing of rights premised on the existence of equal, autonomous individuals becomes an almost impossible exercise. Equality as a value becomes less relevant when we confront communities whose difference to our own overwhelms the hierarchy it reveals. Where there is hierarchy there is power, and the legal system is not equipped to deal with the active exercise of power by one group over another. Thus, when women bring their lives into the courtroom, they issue a fundamental challenge that reaches into the very core of liberal legalism.

It is perhaps because of the revolutionary cast of their activities that women who litigate often describe the technical aspects of their challenge, leaving it to others to evaluate its feminist potential. Lynn Smith, who has litigated on behalf of LEAF in cases involving discrimination on the basis of pregnancy, described her task simply as getting judges to critically exam-ine unstated assumptions about women. For example, the view that preg-nancy is a voluntary condition informs judges' opinions about who should bear responsibility for its consequences. If women choose to have families, this line of reasoning goes, they cannot then expect to have careers. The myths about freedom of choice and autonomy underlie perceptions about the rights of pregnant women. The litigator's task is to identify such assumptions and to challenge them in court. This is not, however, as straightforward as it might seem, and Lynn Smith spoke of "being very careful, not being personal, and not using pronouns that are accusatory." The skill is to find a perspective, an analogy, an example to which men can relate and by which they are not threatened. [50]

Getting men to understand women's reality, to see women's experience as valid, is understandably not without some risks, and it is these risks that perhaps distinguish litigation on behalf of women from some other litigation activities. [51] For one, revealing elements of women's situation in society leads very quickly into a discussion about power and oppression. As Mary Eberts noted, when you "come out with something that speaks more clearly in political science or values terms ... it's not a very large step from there to some of the more explicit feminist positions." Speaking about oppression will require breaking legal rules. For instance, legal discourse structured around comparison (the treating of likes alike) will not be a useful tool with which to grasp the reality of women's oppression since on many points there will be no comparison. Further, if the full implications of women's situation are to be grasped, litigators have to find ways in which to resist the legal narrowing intrinsic to law and to emphasize the social context of the facts under consideration. They also need to strive for solutions that improve the status of women, real-life solutions that cannot be arrived at *unless* the social context is explicitly acknowledged. Finally, speaking of women's reality is threatening – no matter how much care is taken. If, as Mary Eberts found, "the scepticism of the judge goes up directly in proportion to the extent to which he feels threatened by what you're telling him," then women seeking to convey the violence to which they are exposed as a group will encounter substantial resistance.

Women theorizing about the application of feminism to law identified these hazards; the experience of women litigating on behalf of LEAF confirmed their ideas. Litigating on behalf of women lays oppression bare and women would be naive to expect that with understanding comes automatic acceptance. On the other hand, they are obliged to seek out the potential for understanding wherever they can find it, having few alternate routes to genuine equality as women.

CHAPTER THREE

LEAF CASES:
FEMINIST METHOD
IN THE COURTROOM

THE ISSUES that women take into the courtroom typically concern matters of the private sphere and, as such, fit awkwardly into public discourse. In some circles even today, issues concerning the *personal* travails of childbirth and breastfeeding, sexually explicit intimidation by the boss, sexual assault, and abortion are still not appropriate topics for conversation. Often they appear in the courtroom in full scientific dress: women's needs in childbirth become a medical matter; our experience of harassment, a psychological issue; rape, a sociological phenomenon; and reproductive choice becomes an intellectual problem of balancing the rights of someone who has no independent existence against the rights of someone who does. Women's daily, personal experiences of giving birth, working for pay, taking care of children, and of being raped, battered and harassed, enter the courtroom as though by stealth; feminist legal method enters as the accomplice.

Exposing the World as Man-Made:
The Paradigmatic Case

For twelve days in June 1987, the Supreme Court of Ontario heard the case of the Federation of Women Teachers of Ontario (FWTAO) versus Margaret Tomen and the (predominantly male) Ontario Public School Teachers' Federation (OPSTF).[1] LEAF had no direct involvement in the case but had strong ties to FWTAO, who had been one of LEAF's major sources of start-up funding, a "mother" of LEAF in the eyes of its founders.[2] When FWTAO's right to exist as an all-female organization was challenged in court, it naturally turned to Mary Eberts who acted as counsel on the case along with Elizabeth Lennon, the co-chair of LEAF's legal committee in 1988. Their consultants were Catharine MacKinnon and Kathleen Lahey, who both had previously advised and consulted with LEAF. For Mary Eberts, the two and a half years it took to prepare this case were the years during which she developed many of the ideas and the legal approach she would apply to LEAF cases. As she put it, the FWTAO case was for her the "last little bit of throwing caution to the winds."[3] Its relevance to this discussion of feminist method – beyond the connections between FWTAO and LEAF – is that it illustrates how a feminist understanding of the world can be conveyed in court.

The facts of the FWTAO case were simple enough. By-law 1, Section 2(a) of the Ontario Teachers' Federation, of which FWTAO is a member organization, compels all female teachers to pay their dues to FWTAO, thereby constituting a closed shop and an all-female union of teachers. Margaret Tomen, an FWTAO member, wanted the right to opt out of the closed shop, preferring instead to pay her dues to the Ontario Public School Teachers' Federation (OPSTF) – the brother organization of FWTAO which offers memberships to both men and women public school teachers. Women can choose to be members of OPSTF but they remain compelled to pay dues to FWTAO; men, however, are compelled to pay their dues to OPSTF. At the root of Margaret Tomen's complaint was her feeling that the by-law compelled her to join an all-female union that had a "female-ghetto mentality." For its part, FWTAO characterized Margaret Tomen's complaint and the OPSTF challenge as "simply another union raid" disguised as a Charter challenge. FWTAO's numerical and financial superiority, it argued, had tempted OPSTF to try a union takeover in the past, and Tomen's suit was merely the latest attempt in this direction. The impact of acceding to Margaret Tomen's request that By-law I be declared invalid (on the basis that it denied Tomen her freedom of association) would end the closed shop at FWTAO, thereby making its funding base less secure; the same situation would not apply to OPSTF. [4]

The Federation of Women Teachers of Ontario found itself having to defend its role as a union for women only, a defence that had to take into account the importance of the constitutional right to freedom of association and the special conditions under which sex distinctions such as an all women's union are permissible under the Charter of Rights and Freedoms (i.e., as an affirmative action measure under section 15(2)). For Mary Eberts, a justification of FWTAO's right to exist required proof that sex inequality existed in the teaching field and in society and that mixed-sex unions *in this instance* would only serve to deepen it. These broad issues then had to be legally reformulated as Charter issues.

Relying on Supreme Court precedents (i.e., *Oakes, Big M, Edwards Books*), the brief filed by FWTAO outlined a four-part legal argument. First, the by-law did not contravene the Charter and any limits it placed on Margaret Tomen's rights were reasonably justifiable. Second, the Charter was not applicable in this instance because the by-laws of the Ontario Teachers' Federation were not laws or regulations made by government; thus, they could be classified as private not state actions. [5] Third, Tomen's freedom to associate could not be said to be curtailed simply because FWTAO was a closed shop. Canadian law already provided for this exception to freedom of association. Finally, FWTAO urged the court to follow a purposive approach to the interpretation of the Charter, namely, that it pay heed to the purpose of the regulation in question and to the Supreme Court's declaration in earlier cases that the Charter should not be used to advance the interests of dominant groups at the expense of the disadvantaged. [6]

To make an argument in court that sex inequality existed and that mixed-sex union arrangements for Ontario's teachers only served to perpetuate it, was to make an argument framed in terms of women's collective status. Conversely, Margaret Tomen's and OPSTF's claims rested on an individual's right to associate and on the argument that individual women teachers could be found who were equal to individual men teachers. The group perspective relied on the notion of individuals in their social context and community; the individualist perspective depended on a view of the essential autonomy of human beings. Legal discourse favours the individualist view in many different ways. Its raison d'être is the balancing of competing claims between theoretically autonomous individuals – the concept of community and context clashes fundamentally with this premise; group status is less amenable to legal reformulation and to the reduction of conflict to the mode of competing claims. It is also less easily conveyed within the rules of scientific discourse. The individual in her community is a less provable reality than is the individual presumed to have none. Her essence is less easily named, empirically validated, and objectively proven. When that community is further described as disadvantaged or oppressed, its impact on the individual is not only less measurable, but also less palatable. FWTAO had these difficulties to overcome.

The battle in court began, predictably, over statistics. In an affidavit submitted on FWTAO's behalf, the economist Monica Townson introduced statistical evidence that women teachers earned on average less than men teachers.[7] OPSTF disputed her claim, declaring that women with the same number of years of experience as their male counterparts earned the same, as outlined in the collective agreement; whatever differences there were, were due to individual differences. Under cross-examination by Mary Eberts, OPSTF President Mary Hill insisted that women teachers enjoyed equal status to men teachers and made it clear that for her the formal equality enshrined in the collective agreement amounted to substantive equality.[8] Indeed, when the focus was the individual woman, in this case Margaret Tomen, the substantive equality of women as a group was not the issue.

Mary Hill's perceptions of the reality of women teachers certainly reflected the individualist perspective and rejected outright any group emphasis. When Mary Eberts asked her, "You seem to be suggesting that if you can do it, any woman could do it; is that correct?" her reply was a firm "yes."[9] "In my view," Mary Hill had opined in her affidavit, "the best way to learn to compete with men in a professional context is to compete with them in as many other contexts as possible, including the labour union movement."[10] Pressed during the cross-examination to acknowledge that her opinions on the superiority of mixed-sex unions derived from personal experience, Mary Hill again replied yes, as did Ross Andrew, an executive officer of OPSTF, when asked about his statement that the status of women teachers had improved greatly.[11]

With some justification, FWTAO declared in its brief to the court that "the OPSTF tenders no expert evidence and no statistical evidence for its assertion that a dual-sex organization would be equally capable of responding to the concerns of female teachers"; it relies on hearsay evidence and on the single testimony of Mary Hill.[12] OPSTF did, however, invite the head of the Equal Opportunity Department of the National Union of Teachers of England, Jean Farrall, to submit an affidavit describing the beneficial effects of a mixed-sex environment for the women of her union. Farrall's testimony provided the only point on which there could be specific discussion of OPSTF's testimony. For the most part, FWTAO's argument had to remain in the realm of women's group reality and in their common situation as women teachers. To legitimize that reality in the eyes of the court, it introduced a vast array of expert testimony in what appeared to be an all out offensive against the limited scale of Tomen's and OPSTF's presentations.

It took twenty affidavits from experts across a wide variety of disciplines to make the case for an all-female union, a scale made possible by the resources of FWTAO and the international connections of Catharine MacKinnon and Kathleen Lahey in the field of women's studies.[13] Mac-Kinnon's own affidavit set out the direction of FWTAO's argument. Women, she asserted, are a subordinate group in most societies. Members of such groups are "typically paid less well and advanced less regularly and have less social status, resources, security, and respect." Further, she continued,

> there is no legal instrument through which a woman can disaffiliate herself from the group women in society. The community of interest of women as a group will continue to exist, and will objectively include all individual women teachers, so long as their social inequality on the basis of sex remains. In light of this recognition, it would undermine progress toward sex equality to permit an individual woman to require that women as a group, from which no women may exit, may not combine together to defend the interests of all women.[14]

Lorenne Clark, a professor of philosophy, addressed in her affidavit the historical evolution of the concept of equality, noting how women have only recently come to be included in its scope.[15]

Moving from the historical and the general to the specific, and clothing each successive argument in expert and scientific garb, affidavits submitted by FWTAO then took up the meaning of inequality in detail. Margrit Eichler, a professor of sociology, began her submission with an irresistible logic: "the point of having equality guarantees [in the Charter] is to reduce inequalities."[16] She then elaborated ten dimensions of inequality explaining how these factors enable us to quantify inequality and to assess which policies or practices reduce or increase it. Women could measure their inequality by evaluating, for instance, the extent to which they physically survived; had a sense of personal worth; control over property; control over access to society's goods and services; control over their bodies; control over political processes, etc. Applying inequality criteria to FWTAO, Eichler noted that the organization enabled women to have (among other things) a high degree of control over political representation; property (in the form of dues); access to relevant knowledge about their status; access to valued goods and services (for example, it persuaded the Ministry of Education to offer a pre-training program for women wanting to be school principals); and it promoted and enhanced women's self-worth and respect. There was then no question that without FWTAO, women teachers would have little opportunity to change their unequal situation.[17]

Inequality, as described by Margrit Eichler and Catharine MacKinnon was a quantifiable phenomenon not only with respect to pay and employment opportunities but also in the area of such intangibles as self-worth and control over one's social status. The intention, of course, behind this approach was to legitimize, in ways familiar to the court, evidence about women teachers' need to organize autonomously. To drive the point home, FWTAO then introduced both contemporary and historical evidence about what happens to women's concerns in mixed-sex and single-sex groups, and specifically in unions. Two European experts testified, for example, that their governments permitted all-female unions to exist in some sectors, recognizing women's need for affirmative action measures in order to improve their status.[18] It was not unintentional that these particular affidavits should have referred to measures of positive discrimination or affirmative action since Section 15(2) of the Charter of Rights and Freedoms explicitly permitted such programs to exist wherever they can be shown to ameliorate conditions for disadvantaged groups. Alice Cook, well-known for her international work on women and unions, noted that after an early attempt to ban women from unions, men allowed women to become members of unions but "have almost universally neglected to represent their interests and pursue their grievances."[19] Her views were reinforced by Janet Pollack, an activist of Britain's National Union of Teachers (NUT). Pollack specifically refuted the affidavit of Jean Farrall, tendered by OPSTF, noting that the NUT was so unresponsive to the needs of women teachers that women union members organized a special caucus to press for their needs internally.[20]

Mixed-sex unions only replicated relations between the sexes that prevailed elsewhere. Thus, FWTAO introduced affidavits from scholars in women's studies who offered their research findings about male/female behaviour in mixed-sex groupings. Dale Spender noted in her affidavit that "one of the topics of specific interest to women which is routinely controlled or pre-empted by men in mixed-sex groupings is the inequality of women.... Unless women's issues and views are presented in a way which is acceptable to men, women will not be given a proper hearing."[21] In her affidavit, Margaret Littlewood, a research officer of the Centre for Research and Education on Gender at the University of London, England, concurred. Men, she wrote, oppose measures to achieve substantive equality in periods of economic recession.[22] Other scholars, both Canadian and international, such as Margaret Beattie, a political science professor in Quebec who studied teachers' unions in that province, confirmed the disadvantages women suffer in mixed-sex groupings adding that the presence of an all women's organization inevitably enhanced opportunities for women to improve their status.[23] Not content to leave the argument at the level of contemporary research, FWTAO also submitted affidavits from historians. Jill Conway testified that historically men have dominated when they got the chance and that women's institutions have in the past played "a vital role in fostering women's potential."[24] Joy Parr's affidavit matched this view from a Canadian historical perspective. Parr described how equality in law seldom brought Canadian women substantive equality unless they specifically organized as women to protect their rights.[25]

Leaving nothing to chance, FWTAO then took the discussion on to home turf, describing its own historical and contemporary role in improving the status of women teachers. Beginning with the affidavit of Marguerite Cassin, a professor of management studies, testimony began to tear apart any impressions that women teachers currently enjoyed equality. Cassin in particular offered an insightful analysis of how women's present inequality "becomes the mechanism by which future inequality is ensured and intensified."[26] She described "the routine production of inequality in managerial organizations,"[27] for instance, the ways in which women's jobs were structured so that they had limited advancement possibilities.

In the educational setting, job experience, which many women have, was always considered secondary to formal degrees, which women had less chance of acquiring than men did. In recent years, curriculum design has come to be an avenue to career advancement, a qualification normally acquired outside the regular school day, hence less available to women with family responsibilities. Faced with routines based on men's rather than women's realities, women who wanted to advance had to "create social conditions which approximate those of men in order to appear to be committed and valuable teachers, and to be respected as professionals."[28] In this scheme of things, Cassin argued, only exceptional women can survive and these women were unlikely to challenge the gender-based grounds for advancement. In any event, she added, women could not be expected to challenge such arrangements single-handedly. FWTAO provided a critically needed institutional base from which, collectively, women could change the rules.

Cassin's carefully documented description of systemic inequality built into the educational sector, a form of inequality completely unacknowledged in the representations of OPSTF, was then complemented by an equally thorough documentation of FWTAO's historical and contemporary activities. Sylvia Gold, then president of the Canadian Advisory Council on the Status of Women and a previous staff member of the Canadian Teachers' Federation, testified to FWTAO's role in producing women leaders.[29] The assistant deputy minister of education for Ontario responsible for gender equity issues in schools described the leadership role FWTAO played in eliminating sex discrimination in schools.[30] Florence Henderson, a past executive director of FWTAO, detailed the frequent overtures to merge made by OPSTF over the past twenty years, noting that organization's longstanding opposition to affirmative action for women and describing in detail FWTAO's own record on that score.[31] Finally, Joan

Wescott, FWTAO's current executive director, brought the organizational picture painted thus far up to date.[32]

In a feminist use of the courts women endeavour to "flood the market with their own stories."[33] The Federation of Women Teachers of Ontario did just that in its bid to defend the right of women to organize autonomously. Although most of these stories were told in the guise of scientific evidence, that is, as empirically validated facts, ultimately, there remained aspects of women's reality that required, as Mary Eberts commented, a challenge of legal discourse itself.[34] Courts were not in the habit, for example, of hearing such a multi-faceted array of evidence as FWTAO presented. They have not welcomed such an intensely critical assessment of gender relations. Recalling her experience of the FWTAO case, Mary Eberts remembered the tremendous hostility of the presiding judge. The risks, however, were balanced by the advantages of method. Although in the FWTAO's case where the final decision at the level of the Supreme Court of Ontario ignored the evidence at hand and decided that the offending by-law was a private and not a state regulation, hence not actionable under the Charter,[35] it is clear that a court would be hard pressed to disregard such overwhelming testimony about women's experience, particularly in light of the paucity of evidence presented by OPSTF. Several factors affect the outcome of a case, however (as I describe below), not the least of which is how an argument based on a group reality threatens the status quo.

Pregnancy and Childbirth: The Norm will have to Shift

The biological capacity to bear children, it goes without saying, is what most obviously distinguishes women from men. The capacity for pregnancy, therefore, is an immutable sex characteristic and, as LEAF submitted in one of its pregnancy discrimination cases, "the distinction created by pregnancy discrimination is between the gender that has the capacity for pregnancy and the gender that does not."[36] Canadian courts have not always considered pregnancy as intrinsically related to femaleness. In the *Bliss* decision, the court maintained that since not all women get pregnant, the capacity for pregnancy could not be considered to be an immutable sex characteristic. Moreover, women choose to become pregnant, a personal choice for which they must then bear the consequences.

A full decade after *Bliss,* and armed with the equality provisions of the Charter of Rights and Freedoms, LEAF went to court to argue once again that not to take into account women's child bearing responsibilities was to discriminate on the basis of sex. The first case involved Susan Brooks, Patricia Allen, and Patricia Dixon. All three women worked as part-time cashiers at Canada Safeway, a major grocery store chain, and all three became pregnant in 1982. Under Safeway's group insurance plan, a pregnant employee was only eligible for accident/sickness benefits until the tenth week prior to the expected week of confinement. She was then expected to claim maternity benefits offered under the Unemployment Insurance Act, benefits that were lower than any she would have received under the sickness and accident provisions of the group insurance plan. The three women complained to the Manitoba Human Rights Commission that the group insurance plan was discriminatory on the basis of sex; it effectively denied pregnant women sickness and accident benefits for a period of time. The adjudicator appointed to hear the case ruled that the discrimination suffered was on account of pregnancy and not on account of sex and, because pregnancy was not a ground for discrimination under the Manitoba Human Rights Act, dismissed the complaints. The Manitoba Human Rights Commission appealed the adjudicator's decision to the Court of Queen's Bench only to find that the judge in the case agreed with the adjudicator's decision. The case was then taken to the Court of Appeal for Manitoba, where the appeal was also dismissed. In the final stage of its appeal to the Supreme Court of Canada, LEAF applied for and was granted leave to intervene. In its application for intervenor status, LEAF noted that its position was supported by the National Action Committee on the Status of Women, the National Association of Women and the Law, the YWCA, the Ontario Committee on the Status of Women, and the Ontario Advisory Council on Women's Issues. [37]

The case of Christine Marie Davies followed a more direct route through the legal system. Christine Davies applied for and won a position as a secretary-typist with Century Oils. She then informed her new employer that she was pregnant and would have to take maternity leave in two months; Ms Davies was seven months pregnant at the time of her job interview. In response, Century Oils withdrew its offer of employment and Davies complained of sex discrimination to the British Columbia Council of Human Rights. The Council ruled in her favour and awarded her $3600 as compensation for lost wages. When Century Oils appealed the Council's decision to the Supreme Court of British Columbia, LEAF lawyers acted as counsel for Christine Davies.[38]

The first hurdle to cross in convincing the court that pregnancy discrimination amounted to sex discrimination was to convey how women as a group were harmed wherever the reality of pregnancy and child bearing were discounted. LEAF began in *Brooks, Allen, Dixon* by noting that the only persons affected by pregnancy discrimination were women and that a rule or a practice which applied to members of a group who possessed a particular characteristic had the impact of singling out that group for differential treatment.[39] The factum submitted in the case offered this analogy: "To say that pregnancy discrimination is not sex discrimination because there are, at any given time, non-pregnant women, is as illogical as it is to say that discrimination against observant Roman Catholics is not religious discrimination because there are non-observant Roman Catholics."[40] Furthermore, as the Memorandum submitted in the Christine Davies case noted: "The scope of discrimination against women based on their capacity for pregnancy is very broad ... for example, employer questions about the birth control methods and child bearing intentions of perspective female employees."[41] And it added, an estimated 85% of women in the work force will become pregnant at least once in their work life.

For Lynn Smith, LEAF counsel in *Brooks, Allen, Dixon* and the lawyer who had argued the *Bliss* case ten years earlier, there were two unstated reasons why the notion of pregnancy discrimination as sex discrimination had been previously resisted in court. First, pregnancy was considered a voluntary choice, and second, an activity of the private sphere. LEAF's task was therefore to remind the court that pregnancy was often not a voluntary condition and that in any event "the social imperatives for women to bear children are clear and obvious."[42] Pregnancy may happen in the private sphere, but it was no less "productive activity" than work done in the public sphere. Finally, failing to respond to women's child bearing function in society was to impose on women a male norm in employment, a presumption that to participate in paid work one "must forgo childbearing (and perhaps marriage) or operate under a distinct disadvantage."[43]

The Supreme Court of Canada and the Supreme Court of British Columbia both firmly endorsed LEAF's position in the cases of *Brooks, Allen, Dixon* and in *Davies*. In *Brooks, Allen, Dixon* handed down ten years after *Bliss* on May 4, 1989, the Supreme Court of Canada, making reference to points made in LEAF's submissions, decisively laid the issue to rest once and for all:

> Discrimination on the basis of pregnancy is discrimination on the basis of sex. The decision of this Court in *Bliss*, which reached the opposite conclusion, is inconsistent with the Court's approach to interpreting human rights legislation taken in subsequent cases and should no longer be followed. Pregnancy discrimination is a form of sex discrimination simply because of the basic biological fact that only women have the capacity to become pregnant.... Those who bear children and benefit society as a whole should not be economically or socially disadvantaged. It is thus unfair to impose all the costs of pregnancy upon one half of the population.
>
> It is also wrong to believe that pregnancy related discrimination could not be sex discrimination because not all women get pregnant. While pregnancy based discrimination only affects part of an identifiable group, it does not affect anyone who is not a member of the group. Indeed, pregnancy cannot be separated from gender.[44]

In the case of Christine Davies, the presiding judge accepted the view that "discrimination which is aimed at, or has its effect upon some people in a particular group as opposed to the whole of that group, is not any the less discriminatory," and he noted in passing that any more restrictive a view of discrimination "probably runs contrary to societal expectations."[45] Clearly, in pregnancy cases at least, the norm shifted away from men in order to accommodate a biological female reality. When the terrain moved from an obvious biological condition, as it is in pregnancy, to a socially produced one, as in child rearing, LEAF had to make clear to the court where biological imperatives ended and social practices began. It is here that the full meaning of oppression began to be spelled out in court.

Child Rearing

In her work on women and the law, Carol Smart has noted how the law operates to reinforce the patriarchal family to the extent that in individual cases, male plaintiffs may lose if the interests of the family are deemed to be better served by this outcome. That is to say, both men and women have to conform to a patriarchal ideal. [46] In cases involving child rearing, LEAF's success in court is likely to depend on the extent to which patriarchal ideals are challenged, and also, conversely, the extent to which they can be appealed to in the interests of protecting women's rights. In those cases involving child rearing, one can see clearly that judges are more receptive to women's realities, and less receptive to men's, whenever women's claims sustain patriarchal family ideals.

After their divorce, Michael Jacob Klachefsky and Isabel Margaret Brown shared custody of their two children until Isabel Brown accepted a job promotion and moved to another city. Both parents then sought sole custody, with generous access given to the other. Until this event their arrangements had worked well, moving the judges who later presided over the ensuing custody dispute to comment that the case was one of the most difficult they had ever been called upon to decide, both parents having done an extraordinary job of co-parenting. [47] At the first level, the trial judge held in Michael Klachefsky's favour on the basis that although he would normally have chosen Isabel Brown as the superior parent, he was obliged, in the best interests of the children, to select their father who had recently remarried and thus could provide them with home care as opposed to day care arrangements. (The new spouse, then pregnant, planned to stay at home to care for all three children.) Isabel Brown, as a working mother, was obliged to hire a caregiver between the hours of 3:00 p.m. and 5:30 p.m. LEAF applied for and was denied intervenor status when the trial judge's decision was appealed, the Court of Appeal deciding that Isabel Brown's own lawyer could speak to the issues at hand in what was essentially a private dispute. [48]

The final decision rendered in the custody dispute between Isabel Brown and her ex-husband offered some interesting insights into the ideals and assumptions that inform judicial assessments of what constitutes the proper care of children. Two of the three judges involved ruled in favour of

Isabel Brown, noting that in doing so they were not disputing the opinion of the trial judge who considered her the superior parent yet did not award her custody. Commenting on Isabel Brown's previous ability to provide a stable home, The Honourable Mr Justices Huband and O'Sullivan considered it inappropriate to identify home care as superior to day care. As they expressed it, "whether an alternate caregiver is paid or unpaid, cannot be decisive of what is in the best interests of the children."[49] Significantly, they added to this the assessment that in their view Isabel Brown had in the past provided a stable home, in contrast to Michael Klachefsky who, in the course of five years, had had relationships with three women and whose relationship with his current wife was not always a smooth one. The dissenting judge in the case, The Honourable Mr Justice Philp, disagreed strongly with the majority finding of instability. He coupled his concern for the possible erosion of the children's special relationship with their father if they moved with their mother to another city, with the observation that Isabel Brown had "chosen to put her career interests above all else."[50] Thus in both opinions a family ideal was invoked as justification: Michael Klachefsky lost custody because of his failure to conform to the image of the stable, monogamous family man (although the day care/home care issue did play a role); Isabel Brown was condemned for her failure to accept the duties of motherhood before all else, her economic needs notwithstanding. As in a game played with dice, Isabel Brown won because two out of three judges felt she came closest to emulating the family ideal all three justices shared.[51]

The *Brown/Klachefsky* case involved two individuals who closely fit patriarchal norms. Their deviation from the norm, in Isabel Brown's case as a working mother and in Michael Klachefsky's case as a man involved in short-term relationships, pale in comparison to the deviations at issue in some other custody disputes, and it is in these cases that women find themselves at greater risk than men. Women who are lesbians, for instance, find their lesbianism to be more of an issue than their ex-spouses' violent behaviour. Gayle Bezaire lost custody of her children even in light of the evidence that demonstrated her ex-spouse's physically abusive behaviour towards her and the children. Phyllis Chesler, an American feminist called to Canada to testify in the Bezaire case, has written of the trends in American courts toward penalizing women in custody disputes for any deviation from the patriarchal female norm, particularly when that deviation involved sexual orientation. Closer to home, Susan Crean has observed that in Canada women most often lost custody when they were unable to match the material comforts men were able to provide for their children. [52] In such instances, women had to make a compelling argument for their ability to mother, an argument they could not hope to win unless they could appeal to the patriarchal norms operating in judges' minds. LEAF has not yet had an opportunity to sustain such a challenge in the area of child custody.

One can in fact utilize patriarchal assumptions to women's advantage, as LEAF did in the case of *Shewchuk v. Ricard*. Vicki Shewchuk alleged that Jerry Ricard was the father of her child (born out of wedlock) and was thus compelled to pay maintenance until the child was nineteen years old. Jerry Ricard went to court claiming that the British Columbia Child Support and Paternity Act compelled fathers to pay support but did not compel mothers to do so. The provincial court judge assigned to hear the case agreed with Ricard and dismissed Vicki Shewchuk's appeal, noting, however, that the court had no authority at this level to declare the offending statute void. [53]

At the next stage of appeal, the Attorney General of British Columbia argued before the court that the Child Support and Paternity Act did indeed make a distinction between the rights of mothers and fathers, but the distinction "had a rational basis in the differing reproductive roles of males and females. It was directed to meet special conditions – sexual differences in birth and care of the newborn – and to attain a necessary and desirable objective – provision and maintenance of children." [54] The argument, based on biology and the fulfilment of the special needs of mothers, is not without risks as feminists have long maintained. It was not surprising, then, that The Honourable Mr Justice Locke, presiding over the appeal, should have ruled that the Act could be justified as a special program to ameliorate the status of a disadvantaged group, an affirmative action measure conforming to Section 15(2) of the Charter. [55]

The case was further appealed to the British Columbia Court of Appeal and it was here that, in spite of LEAF's intervention, the court made its decision based on assumptions about women's role in child rearing, assumptions born of both a biological and a social female reality. LEAF, according to Lynn Smith who was counsel in the case, had calculated that *Shewchuk v. Ricard* could mean that women would lose their right to sue for child support. At the same time, LEAF counsel trusted in the court's paternalism and in the unpopularity of a plaintiff seeking to avoid his paternal responsibilities, and believed that the court would not be inclined to deprive Vicki Shewchuk of child support, but would look for a solution other than striking down the legislation. On the other hand, the preceding court's solution that the Act was an affirmative action measure was a highly undesirable one because it entrenched the notion that child rearing was solely a mother's responsibility. LEAF counsel, therefore, sought the court's acceptance of the remedy of extension. That is, they hoped the court would broaden the reach of the Child Support and Paternity Act to include both men and women. Few women if any would be affected – they seldom avoided their maintenance responsibilities and were, in any event, easily proven as mothers. Such a remedy would also appeal to those who worked from a premise of gender neutrality, and it would avoid any confusion about the roles of men and women in child rearing. The one difficulty was that Canadian courts were generally unwilling to broaden or read up legislation believing this to be a function of Parliament.

The *Shewchuk v. Ricard* case was decided on May 9, 1986, just over a year after the equality provisions of the Charter had come into effect. This factor may explain why the three judges deciding the case found it difficult to accept LEAF's argument for extending the Act to apply to both men and women. It may be too, as Lynn Smith suggested, that Jerry Ricard's case was not a popular one, and Vicki Shewchuk could appeal to the fullest paternalist sentiments of the court. [56] Two of the three judges declared that the Act did violate Section 15(1) of the Charter, that is, that it did discriminate on the basis of sex. However, both ruled that although the Act could not be justified as an affirmative action measure, as Mr Justice Locke had ruled earlier, it could represent a reasonable limitation on Jerry Ricard's rights given its broader public purpose "to establish paternity and therefore provide a basis for shifting the financial responsibility for the child from the public to the private domain."[57] The majority decision, while it did not embrace LEAF's position on extension, did at least reject the affirmative action justification adopted by the earlier court and did not strike down the law, thereby depriving women of the right to sue for child support. The dissenting opinion of The Honourable Mr Justice Nemetz, however, revealed that LEAF had not managed to protect women entirely from the risks of winning rights based on women's historic and unequal role in child rearing and on their need of protection because of it. There was no discrimination in the Act, Mr Justice Nemetz wrote, because the distinctions made in it were there "because women are biologically different from men and because single women and the children born out of wedlock by them require the maximum protection that can be afforded them."[58] In this opinion, anatomy became destiny, and the social situation of women performing the major tasks of child rearing, became an exclusively female role to be accommodated in law, a precedent women would have been better off without.

"Experiential Evidence of Women's Lives"[59]

There is not always an opportunity to present to judges evidence that would enable them to separate biological from social realities, and still less occasion to press home the point that women's reality is one of oppression. Even if all this were to be accomplished, there is still the task of devising and winning acceptance for "real-life" solutions that actually improve women's lives. The natural resistance of judges to new arguments, their gender-based difficulties with information about women's lives, and finally, the realities of power that stall the transition from legal change to actual policy changes are all constraints that further affect women's success in the courtroom. In the *Schachter* case, where LEAF had an opportunity to introduce evidence, cross-examine, and call witnesses,[60] the potential for change in spite of these obstacles becomes clear. In another case, however, that of the Organizational Society of the Spouses of Military Members (OSSOMM), LEAF's role was much more restrictive and illustrates where the difficulties might lie for women telling their stories in court.

Until LEAF became involved in the case, the suit brought by Shalom Schachter against the Canada Employment and Immigration Commission appeared to have little to do with the experiential dimension of women's daily lives, although the issues it raised had been on the agenda of the women's movement for years. The Unemployment Insurance Act of Canada offered adoptive parents of either sex the right to claim benefits for fifteen weeks beginning with the child's placement in the home, providing the claimant proved that it was reasonable that he or she stay at home to care for the adopted child. The benefit period could not be shared between parents, although clearly, either the adoptive father or mother could apply to be the claimant. The Act also offered a natural mother up to fifteen weeks of benefits, to be taken as she chose, within a period commencing eight weeks before the week of the expected birth and up to seventeen weeks after the week of birth. Except in very limited circumstances, for example the death of a mother (and this only became law in 1988), a natural father was not entitled to benefits for time spent in the care of their new-born child. Shalom Schachter wished to have the right to share his wife's fifteen weeks of leave, since she preferred to return to work shortly after giving birth. He claimed that as a natural father (and thus one similarly sit-uated to an adoptive father), the Unemployment Insurance Act discrim-inated against him on the basis of sex by providing leave for mothers and adoptive parents; therefore, it contravened Section 15(1) of the Charter, the right to the equal benefit and protection of the law.[61] As initially framed, Shalom Schachter's case was, as Mary Eberts put it, "a really clas-sic case of the liberal democratic argument."[62] He claimed nothing more than the right to equal treatment and to a gender-neutral law, resting his case on the foundation that likes must be treated alike. Interestingly, even when LEAF's efforts shifted the focus of the case, the theme of gender neu-trality continued to be its primary appeal for the media as reflected in *The Toronto Star*'s headline "Change 'Biased' Law to Give Dads Benefits, Law-yer Urges Judge."[63]

Starting from the premise that the woman who is pregnant, gives birth, and breastfeeds is *not* similarly situated to natural or adoptive fathers or to adoptive mothers, LEAF's involvement revolved around what would hap-pen to natural mothers who ended up sharing their already meagre fifteen weeks leave. Thus, while entirely in support of Schachter's wish to actively parent and to have the state support him in this role, LEAF intervened to ensure that the leave provisions of natural mothers remained untouched. It suggested the remedy of extension, that is, unemployment insurance ben-efits should be available to all parents, natural or adoptive, *without taking away from the vital leave required by natural mothers.* Proving that natural mothers needed at least fifteen weeks of leave to meet their needs during pregnancy, birth, recovery, and breastfeeding became the alternate activity in the Schachter case, running in a parallel stream beside Schachter's own burden to prove himself similarly situated to adoptive fathers.

The experiential world of pregnancy, birth, recovery, and breastfeeding is the world of the private sphere, an area foreign to scientific discourse and resistant to the conceptual mode of similarly situated. It is a woman's world that cannot be "served up in the impeccably 'objective' sense that male scholarship always tries to assume."[64] To convey the texture of this private world, Mary Eberts drew on the feminist method of the FWTAO case, introducing an array of experts to render women's childbirth experiences scientifically valid, and pressing experts introduced by the other parties to admit women's reality into their conceptual framework, either by acknowledging the natural mother's needs or revealing the gender bias of their views.

We "must consider questions of equality in the context of what actually goes on in people's lives, not just in terms of abstract rights – context is all,"[65] wrote Eberts in her notes for the courtroom trial of the Schachter case. However, the problem for women was, whose context? Did all women, or even most working women, experience the same needs in pregnancy and childbirth, and if they did, how could this be proven in a court of law?

The proof began with Julie Davis, vice-president of the Ontario Federation of Labour (of the Canadian Labour Congress), spokesperson for organized working women. The Canadian Labour Congress officially supported seventeen weeks of leave for the natural mother as an irreducible minimum, and a further twenty-four weeks of parental leave to be taken by either parent and available to natural or adoptive parents. In her affidavit, Julie Davis described how pregnant women working outside the home tried to accommodate their biological needs within the time currently available to them. A study of women taking leave under the Unemployment Insurance Act revealed that 64.2% of women took at least two weeks of their leave before the birth of their child. Describing the physical problems many pregnant women encountered at work, such as exposure to video display terminals, stress, and heavy lifting, Davis noted that women nonetheless usually tried to "bank" their leave in anticipation of their even greater physical needs after birth. Recalling her own experience at a time when no pregnancy benefits existed, she noted: "It was extremely difficult for me to do so (return to work shortly after birth) as I had not recovered from the process of childbirth, was fatigued and was unable to get sufficient sleep."[66]

Referring to this testimony to make her point that women did not use the fifteen weeks of leave strictly for parenting purposes (an assumption of the policy makers), Mary Eberts later reminded the judge that "it would be dangerous and insulting to forget that the women who bear the children are not just bonding in that fifteen weeks – they are often in pain struggling with physical hormonal changes, sleep deprivation, surgery."[67]

Two experts on women's biological needs during pregnancy, childbirth, and breastfeeding confirmed Julie Davis's experience as a mother and as a labour leader. Karyn Kaufman, a professor of the school of nursing and a midwifery expert, and Murray Enkin, an obstetrician with a family-centred maternity care practice, both submitted evidence in their affidavit that the needs of the mother "are separate and in addition to the needs for time for care of the newborn and infant."[68] An internationally renowned expert on health issues affecting women testified that the structure of benefits in most developed countries reflected an acknowledgement of the natural mother's needs. Indeed, Dr Marsden Wagner pointed out that Canada's provisions lagged far behind most European countries who offered to the natural mother more extensive leave, both paid and unpaid, as well as leave provisions to be shared by either parent. The benefit structure that was most common, he explained, acknowledged child bearing as a social responsibility "rather than simply a private decision with private consequences."[69] In cross-examination, Dr Wagner affirmed that he knew of no industrialized country where benefits for natural fathers were at the expense of natural mothers.

Having presented a case for women's biological needs, and having located that case within the context of international norms, LEAF then had to ensure that its position was not contradicted by the experts called by both the Crown and Schachter's lawyers. Thus when Dr George Awad, a child psychologist called by Brian Morgan, Schachter's lawyer, spoke of the importance of father/child bonding, Mary Eberts pressed him to acknowledge that although the father's participation was highly desirable, it should not be at the expense of the mother's.[70] Similarly, when the director general of Unemployment Insurance took the stand, he was cross-examined by Mary Eberts about the rationales behind the current provisions in the Unemployment Insurance Act. For example, pregnant women claiming benefits were required to undergo a waiting period of two weeks before benefits began, the same condition that applied to other unemployed workers. The initial rationale behind the two week waiting period was that it encouraged unemployed workers to look for work, a rationale that would not apply to the pregnant woman who was in fact unavailable for work. Policy decisions, then, often did not reflect the real-life conditions of claimants and, in the case of women, decisions were based on an assessment of women's parenting needs, not on their specific biological role.[71]

The arguments put forward by Brian Morgan on behalf of Shalom Schachter and the opposing arguments of the Crown ran alongside of LEAF's, seldom merging and occasionally flowing in an opposite direction. Since their preoccupation was the concept of similarly situated, a framework was established based on a competition between the claims of natural mothers, natural fathers, and adoptive parents. The Crown attorney, for instance, characterized the purpose of the leave provisions of the Unemployment Insurance Act as income protection for one member of the family surrounding the event of the entry of a new child into the family; that member could be either the mother or the father. Biological needs were not at issue, neither was the issue of a father's right to nurture.[72] Brian Morgan spoke mainly of the inequity that existed when natural fathers were denied benefits, framing the argument in terms of discrimination and leaving the impression, in Mary Eberts's view, that to give the natural mother exclusive leave was to put her in a superior position relative to fathers and adoptive mothers.[73] Weighing competing claims without due regard to the real-life situation of the claimants, therefore, remained the predominant approach of all parties except LEAF.

The Honourable Mr Justice Strayer, in his reasons for judgement in the Schachter case[74] delivered on June 7, 1988, explicitly endorsed the position argued by LEAF. In an unprecedented decision accepting the remedy of extension, he declared that while there clearly was sex discrimination in this instance, sharing benefits would have the practical effect of denying a natural mother her childbirth leave. He emphasized that his conclusion "is predicated on my finding that section 30 benefits (the current 15 weeks entitlement for natural mothers) are essentially for pregnancy and cannot be regarded as of more than incidental use for childcare purposes."[75] LEAF had made its case for women's biological needs, a stunning victory tempered by the federal government's subsequent announcement of its intention to appeal the decision.[76]

The experiential dimension explored in the *Schachter* case, the world of pregnancy and childbirth, while not one that is easily validated and communicated, touches most men's and women's lives at least tangentially. Arguing for the time to recover from the birthing process, Caesarean sections and the physical complications that often occur after birth, the time to establish breastfeeding and to adjust to the psychological impact of caring for a newborn who is so intensely physically linked to its mother, is, in quite a literal way, arguing for motherhood. One would be hard pressed to argue convincingly against it, and indeed Schachter recognized this implicitly when he framed his own claim in terms of a parallel argument for fatherhood. Who can quarrel with the desire to parent? LEAF's accomplishment was in keeping the court focused on the needs of natural mothers and away from the abstract balancing of competing claims. Without minimizing the achievement, one must also recognize that LEAF's position on the difficulties of child bearing was one for which there was much sympathy, although there may not have been a widespread eagerness to view the process as a social responsibility. What happens when the experiential dimension that is presented in court is not nearly so attractive, and is, in fact, a reality to be resisted? Consider the possible courtroom scenario of the Organizational Society of the Spouses of Military Members (OSSOMM).

OSSOMM was incorporated on April 11, 1985, a few days before the moratorium on the equality sections of the Charter was lifted and LEAF came into existence. Its purpose was "to improve the quality of life for spouses of military personnel, educating its members and developing organizational skills for women."[77] OSSOMM's activities included lobbying for a dental care plan for children and a traffic light at a school crossing. Early in its history OSSOMM earned the displeasure of the base commander at the military base at Penhold, Alberta, who felt that OSSOMM's activities were contrary to the regulations of the National Defence Act which prohibited political activities on military bases. The base commander's position was supported by the Minister of National Defence Eric Neilson. Alleging that its members were being denied their freedom of association, and were in addition being discriminated against on the basis of their marital status and sex, OSSOMM took the dispute to court with LEAF's help, filing a statement of claim in the Federal Court of Canada on January 13, 1986.

Defending the position of the Ministry of National Defence, the Deputy Attorney General Frank Iacobucci declared in his statement that "the stated aims and objectives of the plaintiffs, or some of them, included objectives which can best be attained through legislative, regulatory, administrative, or financial action by elected representatives of the municipal, provincial or federal government."[78] OSSOMM held "political meetings," conducted door-to-door delivery of their newsletter and engaged in "delivering a political speech." Further, in asking those who supported the idea of a dental plan to mail a pre-prepared card to the Prime Minister, OSSOMM engaged in lobbying, a prohibited activity on a military base.[79]

A Special Senate Committee on National Defence took up the issue of political activities on military bases and its proceedings, at which LEAF appeared, offer a rare glimpse into the underlying motivations and fears behind opposition to OSSOMM. In his appearance before the committee, the new Minister of National Defence Harvie André made a very careful distinction between lobbying and political activity, the latter requiring in his view the use of "political muscle," a quality he attributed to OSSOMM.[80] Mr André was particularly explicit about the nature of OSSOMM's offence. What we (the government) do not allow, he stated, is an organization whose role it is "to challenge the chain of command, to challenge the authority of the military, to challenge the authority of base commanders." OSSOMM should confine its role, he opined, to one of requesting the authorities to make the appropriate changes.[81] When pressed by the presiding senator to identify what recourse military wives might have should the base commander say no to their requests, Mr André replied:

> You cannot have recourse without having, in essence, a challenge to that authority (the base commander's). If someone does not have to accept the authority, they can bypass it. If they can bypass it, they are immediately challenging the chain of command. You cannot have the two.[82]

LEAF, appearing before the committee in OSSOMM's defence, suggested that OSSOMM seemed to be in trouble "for looking as though they really mean it," if one was to go by the testimony of the Minister of National

Defence. When asked to explain exactly why it would be inappropriate for military husbands to take up issues on their wives' behalf, LEAF's litigation director politely replied: "It does not seem right to me that an adult should have to rely upon another adult in the exercise of her democratic freedom."[83] She then went on to outline how restrictions on OSSOMM amounted to treating military wives as appendages of their husbands, treatment that offended the equality provisions of the Charter of Rights and Freedoms.

When women organize autonomously to press for their demands, as the women of OSSOMM and FWTAO did, what are they saying? Ann Scales, writing of the military context, offers some interesting insights on the incompatibility of feminism and militarism that shed light on what may have been at issue in OSSOMM's case. "Feminism," she writes, "cannot countenance the violence and divisiveness that militarism requires, nor the view of the world that allows it."[84] That world view is one that relies on hierarchy, on the unquestioned submission to authority of both women and men. There is a strong gender component to the hierarchy, however, that in the case of the military is singularly obvious. As Scales elaborates, militarism needs women in various functions. Above all, "it needs us to have *no* political authority so that our only choice is to grieve, to ventilate the ugliness of the enterprise."[85] Significantly, militarism

> enforces a way of looking at the world that oppresses individual women. Militarism supplies the moral authority for relations of dominance and submission.[86]

When individuals "are led to think they have no choice, that they are merely conforming to an absolute authority outside themselves," Scales observed, the foundation is laid for domination and tyranny. Thus, "the militaristic individual feels justified in forcing others to submit to his unquestionable values and authority."[87] In the same vein, Cynthia Enloe has written in *Does Khaki Become You?* of how "the military has employed a variety of notions of 'the family' in order to control both the men and the women it needs to achieve its goals."[88]

That the women of OSSOMM lived exactly the reality described by Scales and Enloe became clear in OSSOMM's testimony before the Senate Committee. Leslie V. Taylor, an OSSOMM member, described for the committee the five most important areas of concern to military families: postings, father/husband absences, alcohol as a symptom of lifestyle stress, family privacy, and "our feeling about the military."[89] She spoke movingly of the emotional upheaval frequent moves cause military families and explained why military wives "do not enjoy having our thinking done for us, or of having no voice in family and social issues." Attempting to convey the tenor of her daily life, Leslie Taylor noted: "Service members sometimes have a hard time leaving their hierarchical place of work to go to a democratic structure in the home."[90] In her testimony, Lucie Richardson, OSSOMM's president, was more explicit. She described the almost total domination of women by men in the military, from the more benign example of mothers not being authorized to sign for their children's library books to incidents of wife assault on bases. Her testimony also revealed the ridicule, threats, and intimidation to which OSSOMM members were exposed once their political intentions became clear. Initially dismissed and told to go back to their soap operas, OSSOMM women were later threatened with arrest and eviction from the base, and warned of the consequences for their husbands if they spoke out.[91]

When relationships of domination and submission are so revealed, when the experiential dimension conveys the violence in women's daily lives, the telling of women's stories in court becomes risky. That is, it becomes more difficult to be heard and there can be repercussions. OSSOMM women faced threats and found themselves denied a $5000 grant from the Secretary of State, a grant that was intended to sustain the organization itself as a legitimate women's organization.[92] Both the military and the government continued to reject and to belittle OSSOMM's claims. A report commissioned by the Minister of National Defence on the regulation of political activities on military bases described OSSOMM as an "adversarial and frequently antagonistic organization" and proposed meeting OSSOMM's demands by allowing political meetings in homes only and establishing a Canadian Forces family association "to study and suggest solutions to social problems affecting military families." Such an organization, the report suggested, would qualify for financial support on the condition that it accepted a non-partisan role.[93] Feminist method in court has to take into account this and other forms of resistance to the telling of women's stories.

CHAPTER FOUR

Naming Oppression:
issues of domination
and submission

F EW ISSUES bring sexual politics and gender hierarchy into the open as
do sexual harassment and rape. There is an unmistakable "gender
dimension" clinging to both since, by and large, it is men who sexually
harass and rape women. The newer gender-neutral terms notwithstanding, wife assault, incest, and the physical and mental abuse of children also
carry the same stigma: they are what *men* do to women and children. It is
inevitable, then, that when these issues come into the courtroom, they
bring with them a pandora's box of gender relations. They make it less feasible to talk of individuals, to weigh their competing claims as though they
were equal, and to ignore the social realities in which they operate. The
issues of sexual harassment, rape, wife assault, incest, and child abuse
require context, not just of the individual plaintiff and respondent but of the
gender to which each belongs.

To raise the issues of sexual violence and domination in the courtroom
and in a feminist way is to name women's oppression and to insist on its relevance. There is not, however, "a failsafe way for women to inform men of
their perspective"; one has to strike a balance between "bold subversion

and wise restraint."[1] Standing in the way are the legal rules and concepts that narrow experience and reduce its application to cases. There is too, as Boyle reminds us, "an apparent lack of knowledge of how women experience reality."[2] Women who litigate must fill this knowledge gap and, at the same time, challenge the legal rules that would declare it inadmissible. The first case discussed in this chapter is LEAF's challenge of similar situation, a legal rule which, in the past, has impeded women from securing recognition of the oppressive realities that make up their daily lives. Next, cases involving sexual harassment and violence against women are examined. It is in these instances that the domination of men over women is most revealed, and women's success in court depends on the extent to which they can establish this link between sex and power, showing how gender and sexuality construct and are constructed by a fundamental power imbalance between women and men. Finally, cases involving women's control over reproduction – an extremely important area for women and one where women can apply their own woman-centred perspectives to rights in law – are considered.

Andrews v. The Law Society of
British Columbia: The Watershed Case

Mark David Andrews's[3] bid to practice law in the province of British Columbia without fulfilling the Law Society's regulation that practising lawyers be Canadian citizens attracted LEAF's interest when two lower courts ruled against him. The Honourable Madam Justice McLachlin (as she then was), writing the later decision for the British Columbia Court of Appeal, made some pronouncements on the interpretation of Section 15(1) and particularly on its relationship to Section 1, under which limits on rights may be justified if they are deemed to be reasonable limitations in a free and democratic society. Her decision sent Attorneys General in most provinces, as well as a number of groups representing the disadvantaged, scrambling to apply for intervenor status in the case.[4] The intervenors were particularly anxious to argue against the position expressed by Madam Justice McLachlin, thereby contributing to the creation of a precedent more favourable to the interests of women and minorities.

Any court called upon to determine whether an individual's equality rights under the Charter have been denied is faced with assessing whether the distinction made between that individual and others is reasonable. In *Andrews,* the Law Society of British Columbia made a distinction between the right of citizens and non-citizens to practice law in that province. It justified the differential treatment meted out to Andrews, a non-citizen, by claiming, among other reasons, that lawyers often filled positions of responsibility in the government of Canada and that in any event individuals like Andrews only had to wait three years before applying for citizenship. Andrews sought to have the courts declare the distinction irrelevant to the practice of law and thus a denial of his right to equal treatment, as guaranteed by Section 15(1).

At issue in equality rights cases is whether the legitimacy of unequal treatment, that is, the legitimacy of making a distinction on the basis of a group characteristic, is to be tested under Section 15 or Section 1. Section 15 determines whether or not the practice in question provides the equality in and under the law and the equal protection and benefit of the law as guaranteed under Section 15. Section 1 determines whether the denial of the right to equality was a reasonable limitation in a free and democratic society. There are, as The Honourable Mr Justice Strayer explained in his judgement of the *Schachter* case, important conceptual and practical differences depending on the route chosen:

> if it is to be tested under Subsection 15(1) the Court is really thereby defining the scope of the rights guaranteed by that subsection; if the test is conducted under Section 1, this means that a right has been infringed and one is then engaged in determining the validity of the infringement or limitation by the standards of Section 1. There is also an important practical difference: he [sic] who alleges infringement of a Subsection 15(1) right has the onus of showing by a balance of probabilities that such right exists and has been infringed; whereas once this infringement is established, it is the party who is nevertheless relying on the validity of the infringing law who has the burden of justifying it under section 1.[5]

In opting to test the validity of the distinction made by the Law Society of British Columbia under Section 15(1), Madam Justice McLachlin proposed to evaluate first whether or not Andrews had suffered discrimination and second whether or not the discriminatory practice was reasonable, an analysis to be performed within the language of Section 15 and before assessing the claim under Section 1. The onus, therefore, was on Andrews rather than the Law Society to prove that his right to equality had been denied.

LEAF's first objection to the decision was that the precedent gave to the person whose rights were allegedly denied the lion's share of the evidentiary burden. LEAF women had repeatedly stressed the need to get out of Section 15 and into an analysis under Section 1 (for example, the equality approach advocated by Anne Bayevsky and Mary Eberts, and by Lynn Smith in her article in *Righting the Balance*); although, as Mary Eberts in particular recognized, getting out of Section 15 was not that easy. Cases involving practices that indirectly discriminated against women, for example, were hard to prove as *prima facie* instances of a denial of equality rights. LEAF, however, worked out its own approach to the preliminary assessment of rights claims under Section 15(1) and it is on this score that it entertained a second objection to the McLachlin decision.

In Madam Justice McLachlin's view, laws invariably made distinctions and in order to assess which distinctions were valid the court should be guided by the principle of similar situation. The Crown argued that Andrews, a non-citizen, was not in the same situation as a citizen because he was less likely to be acquainted with the customs of Canadian society, among other things. It was permissible (reasonable), therefore, to treat such differently situated persons differently. Further, to test this hypothesis one had to evaluate whether or not the distinction in question (citizenship) was reasonable, weighing its purpose (ostensibly, familiarity with Canadian society) against its impact (denial of employment to non-citizens wanting to practice law) and keeping in mind the right of the legislature to pass laws for the good of all. In its factum on the *Andrews* case, LEAF pointed out the fallacy contained in the similarly situated rule and its inherent dangers for women and minorities. Men and women were usually not similarly situated, it reminded the court, so that to rely on this standard in order to determine whether or not there had been a denial of equality would considerably prejudice the claims of women and others who could not fit the rule.[6] LEAF then offered its own approach to the balancing of claims, an approach predicated on the status of the individual in Canadian society, a status based on his or her group characteristic.

Section 15's equality rights had a specific litigable context and history which LEAF pressed the court to take into account. Section 15's existence was a reminder of the importance of equality as a fundamental value. Canadian courts, according to LEAF, already accepted the importance of certain groups' equality claims, and LEAF declared, the Charter was not to be used to roll back these claims. Further, courts already supported "increasing the substantive equality of those groups previously excluded from power and full participation in society."[7] The history of the equality guarantees in the Charter clearly indicated who such groups were. LEAF defined them as groups who *historically* have been denied power "because of the adverse effects of apparently 'neutral' forms of social organization premised on the subordination of certain groups and the dominance of others." Lest there be any confusion in the court's mind as to the defining characteristics of the groups intended to be the beneficiaries of the Charter's equality guarantees, LEAF announced its intention to refer to them throughout its submission as "the powerless, the excluded, the disadvantaged."[8]

With this historical context in mind, LEAF outlined the balancing-of-rights approach it advocated in place of the procedures supported by Madam Justice McLachlin. The court should assess whether a claim brought under Section 15(1) involved questions of substantive inequality, a focus LEAF counsel Mary Eberts stressed as different from the discrimination approach adopted in the lower courts. A serious claim under Section 15 should relate either to one of the enumerated grounds (such as race, sex or marital status) or to practices "institutionalized throughout society so as to affect, in a systematic and cumulative way, dignity, respect, access to resources, physical security, credibility, membership in community or power." These were indices of inequality, and LEAF was asking the court to evaluate whether or not a practice deepened or relieved inequality for certain specified groups. The inequality approach mandated this kind of group perspective whereas the discrimination approach focused on the individual and on evaluating whether or not his or her claim was reasonable in light of the specific legislation and practice in question. Once an applicant has shown how his or her rights claim meets these criteria, the court should then accept that a denial of rights has occurred and the analysis should switch to Section 1, where its reasonableness is evaluated, thereby relieving the applicant of the burden of proof and placing it on the party denying the right.[9]

The thrust of its arguments, LEAF made clear, was to ensure that Section

15(1) fulfilled the function for which it was intended, namely, to secure equality for those groups historically denied it. As Mary Eberts stated in her address to the court, Section 15 "is aimed at helping those individuals who have been impeded by the view society takes of their group."[10] Aware that this amounted to a radical departure from the court's usual liberal democratic and, therefore, individualist orientation, she took care to argue that the individual versus the group dichotomy was, in fact, a false one. No individual exists without his or her group context, and Eberts urged the court to reject a "concept of rampant individualism which would have the individual with no nets or supports."[11] In the case of women, as dramatically outlined in LEAF's factum, the group context was one of disadvantage:

> Widely acknowledged indices of second class citizenship which have led to the recognition that women are a disadvantaged group include women's unequal pay, allocation to disrespected work, demeaned physical characteristics; targeting for rape, domestic battery, sexual abuse as children and systemic sexual harassment; depersonalization, use in denigrating entertainment, and forced prostitution. For women, these abuses occur in an historical context characterized by disenfranchisement, preclusion from property ownership, exclusion from public life, and a sex-based poverty and devaluation of women's contributions in all spheres of social life which continue down to the present day.[12]

Other intervenors in the *Andrews* case retained the discrimination perspective adopted by the lower courts, although they quibbled over the validity test under Section 15 and some, notably Ontario's Attorney General, also criticized the similar situation rule.

Buried under the legal rubble of the lower court decisions in *Andrews* was a world view of individuals independent of their social context and community. Courts do assess the context of a case, but typically in reference to the specific fact situation under consideration. What LEAF was asking the court to do in the case was to approach its traditional tasks of balancing claims with due regard to an individual's group situation (in this instance, non-citizens). When that group situation is described as oppression or disadvantage, nothing could be more revolutionary in a court of law.

LEAF women were themselves aware of the implications of *Andrews* as their first case to reach the Supreme Court of Canada. When asked about the radical language in the factum LEAF submitted, Beth Atcheson suggested that it represented LEAF's "sense of confidence." Marilou McPhedran noted that three years before, at the time of LEAF's founding, she would not have used the word "oppression" as freely as it was used in *Andrews*. [13] And, in an interview a few months before the Supreme Court of Canada rendered its decision, Mary Eberts responded to a question about her future participation in LEAF this way:

> In the foreseeable future, I will be involved in LEAF but the extent of my commitment depends on what the Supreme Court does in *Andrews*. It's as simple as that for me. That will be a big watershed for us, and for me personally, because if the Supreme Court closes the door on some of the things we want to do, then I think we will all have to reassess what LEAF is doing and what LEAF can do. If the Supreme Court opens the door on the kinds of arguments we want, then I think we have to get into some tough cases that we've been talking about, like the victims of sexual assault. [14]

The decision in *Andrews* was handed down on February 2, 1989, and its significance relayed to an uncomprehending public across the front pages of most major Canadian newspapers. As *The Toronto Star* headlined it, "High Court Launches New Legal Era With Equality Ruling." [15] Of the six Supreme Court justices who heard the case, four decided that the citizenship rule imposed on lawyers in British Columbia was an unreasonable limitation on Mark David Andrews's right to practice law, and two dissented. Their reasons had to do with whether lawyers played a central function in the government of this country and whether citizenship was a valid requirement for those playing such a role. The question of the role of lawyers is not pertinent to this discussion, but it should be noted in passing that here once again a legal decision is presented as a scientific one backed up by precedent when, in fact, the court simply picked its own rationalizations to support its conclusions. What is relevant in the *Andrews* judgement, however, is the court's unanimous articulation of those principles and approach to equality contained in LEAF's submission. In both the majority decision of The Honourable Madam Justice Wilson and the dissenting one written by Mr Justice McIntyre, there was a firm acceptance of the view that Section 15 was intended to protect the rights of groups historically and currently disadvantaged in Canadian society. Non-citizens, for both justices, fell into the category of the powerless and the historically disadvantaged. To illustrate that non-citizens were historically discriminated against, Mr Justice McIntyre made reference in his judgement to laws that in the past have infringed upon the rights of non-citizens. It was in his dissenting opinion, however, that one finds unambiguous support for LEAF's views.

The similar situation rule in particular was firmly rejected by him as a restatement of Aristotle's principle of formal equality (where likes must be treated exactly alike); a principle, he suggested, with so little validity that it could even be used to justify the obvious injustice of Adolf Hitler's Nuremberg laws, which treated all Jews identically, that is, all were to be persecuted.[16] Indeed, Mr Justice McIntyre explicitly noted that Canadian jurisdictions had now progressed beyond *Bliss,* where similar situation was used to support the view that pregnant women were not entitled to the same unemployment insurance benefits as other workers. Equality, he stated, was a positive right. The Charter's equality provisions had "a large remedial component" in that they required the legislature to take positive measures to improve the status of disadvantaged groups. Finally, the McIntyre opinion also indicated considerable support for LEAF's understanding of inequality as a systemic problem arising out of practices that no one individual may have intended, and here again the majority of the court agreed with him. In his words,

> discrimination may be described as a distinction, whether intentional or not but based on grounds relating to personal characteristics of the individual or group which has the effect of imposing burdens, obligations, or disadvantages on such individual or group not imposed on others, or which withholds or limits access to opportunities, benefits, and advantages available to other members of society.[17]

LEAF's position on how the Charter should be interpreted also found support in the *Andrews* judgement. Both Madam Justice Wilson and Mr Justice McIntyre agreed that any limitation on rights must be made under Section 1, thereby placing the onus on the state to justify those laws that deny rights to certain individuals or groups. That the court should respect the wisdom of the legislature in passing certain laws and regulations was also explicitly rejected. The Charter, the court reiterated, was intended precisely to challenge laws that deny rights and that have been passed by legislatures.[18]

With the Supreme Court's decision in *Andrews,* remarked *The Toronto Star* in an editorial, "the less equal can expect to have a better day in court."[19] LEAF had this remarkable achievement to build upon in its subsequent litigation efforts on behalf of women. Its legal work also had a more solid analytical foundation. The factum submitted in *Andrews,* which resulted from considerable workshopping, unambiguously directed the court to the view that women were not similarly situated, that they were in fact *oppressed. Andrews* was not a case about women's daily reality, however, except in so far as LEAF referred to it to make its point. In the cases of *Janzen/ Govereau, Seaboyer/ Gayme,* and *Canadian Newspapers,* which *were* about women's experiences as victims of harassment and rape, the approach used in *Andrews* was put forward once again, revealing its contrast to an individualist, rights-balancing perspective and confirming LEAF's growth into an explicitly radical and feminist organization.

Sexual Harassment

Diana Janzen and Tracy Govereau were waitresses who were sexually harassed by their superior, a cook in the restaurant where they worked. An adjudicator of the Manitoba Human Rights Commission found that there had been harassment, that the complainants had indeed suffered devastating consequences, and that they had been obliged to work in a "poisoned work environment."[20] Nevertheless, at the next level of appeal, the presiding judge of the Manitoba Court of Appeal declined to consider sexual harassment as sex discrimination, basing his view on his assessment that what occurred between the women and their superior had more to do with the cook as an individual being attracted to two other individuals than with his gender or that of his female employees. Furthermore, the cook did not intend his actions to discriminate against women as a group, actions which the court clearly did not take seriously, describing them as akin to a schoolboy stealing kisses.[21] When the case was once again appealed, this time to the Supreme Court, LEAF intervened to protest the basis of the lower court decision and to make clear that sexual harassment is gender-based harm.

In *Janzen/Govereau* LEAF spelled out how sexual harassment fed on men's economic and sexual dominance over women. Sexual harassment, it stated, "both mirrors and reinforces a fundamental imbalance of power between men and women in the workplace and in society," and it was within the context of this power imbalance that the meaning of male and female was socially constructed. Men were socialized one way and women another, and each gender construct fed on the inequality of the sexes. Thus, men were generally in an economically superior position to women and socialized to dominate—men "aggressively initiate sexual interchanges with women, often heedless of women's desires."[22] Moreover, men were conditioned to find female powerlessness and submission erotic. In the workplace even men who did not hold economic power over women used "sexual harassment as a tool for maintaining dominance." Citing studies of sexual harassment, LEAF maintained that in employment it was "pandemic." "Sexual harassment would rarely occur if women and men were social equals,"[23] LEAF concluded.

Characterizing sexual harassment as a feature of men's relations with women, due to the former's power and the latter's powerlessness, is for a court an abstraction, a hypothesis based on the premise that what happens to individual women in cases of harassment happens because of their membership in the group women. LEAF therefore emphasized in its submission in the *Janzen/Govereau* case that to consider the issue of sexual harassment appropriately, the court was obliged to dispense with its custom of similar situation and with an individualist and abstract balancing of claims because the social construction of gender biased the situation of women considerably. LEAF also took care to stress that merely because there was no clear intent to discriminate, and the acts in question were not directed at all women, it did not mean that sex discrimination had not taken place. All women were potential victims of harassment, just as all men were potential harassers because of the power imbalances between the two and because of the role that sexuality played in its expression.

In the case of *Andrews v. the Law Society of British Columbia*, LEAF had won a rare chance to confront the legal rule of similar situation and the myth of the autonomous individual without the explosive context of rape or sexual harassment. The outcome in *Andrews* suggested that there may well be cracks in law's insistence on similar situation and on its exclusive focus on the rights and autonomy of the individual. It was from this point of departure that the court considered the *Janzen/ Govereau* case and rendered its judgement on May 4, 1989. It declared unambiguously that only female employees ran the risk of sexual harassment. The employer Platy Enterprises had attempted to argue that the sole factor underlying the harasser's behaviour was the individual attractiveness, and not the sex, of the two waitresses. Rejecting this outright, the court concluded: "Sexual attractiveness cannot be separated from gender."[24] Further, by accepting many of LEAF's authorities (including Catharine MacKinnon and Constance Backhouse) and crediting LEAF directly, the court indicated its understanding of sexual harassment as an experience women have because they are women, and, therefore, are members of a group who typically fill the least-compensated, least-powerful, and lowest-status jobs in society. There could have been no clearer connection made between sexual harassment and sex inequality and no stronger expression of a group-rights perspective than that made in the Supreme Court's decision in *Janzen/ Govereau*.

Sexual Assault

Rape has long been an issue on which women and men, to put it mildly, have had different perspectives. Understanding the basis to this difference has been the focus of considerable feminist research. In the *Seaboyer/ Gayme* and *Canadian Newspapers* cases, LEAF was required to clarify its own understanding of violence against women and, in turn, to make clear to the court women's experience of it. The two cases offered for judicial scrutiny certain common assumptions about women's situation and about male and female sexuality, assumptions which LEAF explored through cross-country workshops in conjunction with a coalition of feminist groups.[25]

The Supreme Court of Ontario (Toronto Weekly Court) first heard the case of Steven Seaboyer and Nigel Gayme on November 14, 1985.

Seaboyer was accused of raping a woman, whom he had met in a downtown tavern, in his residence. At a preliminary inquiry, his lawyer attempted to cross-examine the woman complaining of rape about her past sexual life. The presiding judge intervened in protest citing Sections 246(6) and 246(7) of the Criminal Code, which prohibited as evidence information about the sexual activity of the complainant with any person other than the accused and which declared inadmissible evidence of sexual reputation for the purpose of undermining the credibility of the complainant. Nigel Gayme, accused of sexually assaulting a fifteen-year-old girl in a school basement, was also prohibited from using the past sexual history of the complainant. Both men then applied to have the relevant sections of the Criminal Code quashed on the basis that they were denied their right to a fair trial as provided for under the Charter.[26] The court accepted their arguments,[27] and the Crown appealed the case to the Court of Appeal of the Supreme Court of Ontario, at which point LEAF intervened.

LEAF's first intervention in *Seaboyer/Gayme* (discussed in chapter two) was an instance where the absence of consultation with the feminist community had resulted in an analysis lacking in feminist content, yet LEAF demonstrated why the rape shield provisions of the Criminal Code, Sections 246(6) and 246(7), were essential for women's equality. The decision rendered by the Court of Appeal supported LEAF's position. In his decision, The Honourable Mr Justice Grange recalled the two assumptions that had led to the admissibility of a complainant's past sexual history – that an unchaste woman was more likely to consent to intercourse and was less likely to tell the truth about it. He explicitly rejected these assumptions, noting that Parliament itself did so when it passed the rape shield provisions. In his view, "sexual reputation is no more an indicator of credibility in a woman than it is in a man." Although he conceded that there might be instances where past sexual conduct was relevant, Mr Justice Grange felt them to be rare enough as to be better left to the determination of the presiding judge. The judge dissenting in this case, The Honourable Mr Justice Brooke, based his opinion on just this issue. In his view, instances where previous sexual history was relevant were not all that rare; he, therefore, supported quashing the rape shield provisions.[28]

Steven Seaboyer and Nigel Gayme's cases are still in court, giving LEAF a second chance in the case to present women's perspectives on the rape shield laws and to do so from the basis of extensive community consultation. As Christie Jefferson noted in an interview, the issue is no longer one which LEAF can claim to take up on its own; rather, LEAF is now part of a coalition of groups supporting legal action on the issue. The *Seaboyer/Gayme* cases were appealed to the Supreme Court of Canada and a decision is pending at the time of writing (November 1990). In the meantime, the Alberta Court of Appeal has ruled that rape shield provisions do violate the rights of the accused to a fair trial, a decision which may also be appealed.

In an affidavit to the court asking for intervenor status in the *Gayme* challenge, LEAF, as part of the feminist coalition it drew together, indicated to what extent its analyses of the construction of women's and men's sexuality and the impact of rape on women had developed since the first *Seaboyer/Gayme* intervention. Based on the benefit of its work done in *Andrews* and its considerable community consultation, LEAF offered this analysis of the impact of rape on women and of the relationship between sexual assault and sex equality:

> Rape violates women physically and mentally, humiliates them, devastates their sense of self-respect, undermines their dignity, and often leaves them with a sense of inferior status in the community which may never be undone. *Threat of rape makes threat of such violation a permanent feature of the landscape of women's lives.*
>
> It is submitted that sexual assault is an equality issue.... Women are singled out for sexual assault and their accusations of sexual assault are systematically disbelieved because of their gender, that is, because they are relegated to an inferior social status as female, including being socially defined as appropriate targets for forced sex....
>
> It is submitted that in an equal society, sexual assault on women and children would be exceptional, rather than as common as it is under current conditions of inequality.[30] (emphasis added)

To substantiate its views, LEAF identified and critiqued prevailing assumptions about women's sexuality and showed how they were sustained in a context of women's social inequality. In *Gayme,* it itemized these assumptions as follows: "children secretly desire to have sex with adults; women secretly desire to have forced sex with men; some children are congenitally promiscuous; if a woman ever has sex with a man, no subsequent sexual event, however forcible, violates her; children fabricate sexual allegations which they cannot distinguish from fantasy; women consent to forced sex and fabricate allegations of coercion to cover their sexual indulgences."[31]

Such assumptions about the behaviour of women and children were particularly relevant in the *Gayme* case since Nigel Gayme wished to use in his defence "mistake of fact," that is, he alleged that he honestly believed his victim consented, a view sustained by her past sexual activity. The crime, if such a defence was used, would be defined according to the accused's beliefs and not according to the victim's experience. This defence was available only if the accused's beliefs were based on events surrounding the alleged rape itself and not on events surrounding other instances of sexual activity. If he was able to use the mistake-of-fact defence in reference to the victim's past history, Nigel Gayme would have succeeded in considerably broadening the current exemptions to the rape shield provisions.

In making the link between inequality and rape, and in bringing to light the underlying assumptions of women's sexuality and character, LEAF has mounted a full-scale challenge of the rape shield provisions. Indeed, the task has been so daunting that it has found itself embroiled in discussions within the coalition. While most members of the coalition have felt strongly that exceptions to the provisions (there are three) were undesirable, there has been some disagreement on how far feminists can go at the present time in their attempt to challenge these exceptions. Disagreement has centred on how much women can afford to risk; a full-scale challenge might well result in a court ruling that the rape shield provisions should be quashed entirely. Further, LEAF has felt limited by the legal requirements that a challenge of this scope would present. For example, a plaintiff has to be found who can provide a fact situation that would enable a successful challenge of the current rape shield provisions. LEAF would also prefer to be proactive rather than reactive, that is to be able to frame its own case rather than to remain tied to the fact situations of a case brought by two alleged rapists.[32]

Feminists have long criticized the male bias of the rules embedded in rape laws, noting, for instance, that the laws have turned on the issue of how much force was used, non-consent being measured by how much the woman physically resisted her attacker. Susan Estrich, writing of rape by an assailant known to the victim, described what she considers to be a male rape fantasy that has underlain rape laws:

> The male rape fantasy is a nightmare of being caught in the classic, simple rape. A man engages in sex. Perhaps he's a bit aggressive about it. The woman says no but doesn't fight very much. Finally she gives in. It's happened like this before. But this time is different: she charges rape. There are no witnesses. It's a contest of credibility, and he's an accused rapist. [33]

For Estrich, the requirements of the law – including force, resistance, corroboration, and fresh complaint – apply equally to all rapes, but in practice are most conscientiously applied to the cases of "simple rape." Thus, women who go to court accusing someone they know of rape run headlong into the power of the male rape fantasy. Such women seldom get to court, Estrich reminds us, since simple rapes, including date rapes, are seldom reported. To be sure the law has well-defined rationales for each of its rules, but Estrich and others have pointed out the practical impact of such rules. For instance, when a woman accuses a man she knows of rape, the court's view has been that the issue is a private dispute. There is, too, an assumption that consent is probably given in such cases and that, in any event, rape by someone you know is less terrifying than rape by a stranger. [34]

All these assumptions ignore the reality of the very real power imbalances that exist between men and women. For those who insist that the law must still protect the man unjustly accused (most commonly, in the fantasy, a vindictive ex-lover) and who frame their argument in terms of equal rights (the man's right to a fair trial versus the woman's right to security of the person), Estrich has an answer:

> For myself, I am quite certain that many women who say yes to men they know, whether on dates or on the job, would say no if they could. I have no doubt that women's silence sometimes is the product not of passion and desire but of pressure and fear. Yet if yes may often mean no, at least from a woman's perspective, it does not seem so much to ask men, and the law, to respect the courage of the woman who does say no and to take her at her word. [35]

Estrich, like many feminists, is asking that we allow for what happens to gender relations in a climate of inequality. Asking that the law take women at their word goes one step further, however, for it also means that not only do we question men's stories, but that we give the benefit of the doubt to women. In a court of law and in a society heavily imbued with the ethic of liberalism and rights discourse (an ethic that has difficulty even with the notion of inequality as a group condition) this request is unlikely to be accepted.

From the first appeals, Nigel Gayme and Steven Seaboyer won the support of the Canadian Civil Liberties Association and individuals endorsing an individual rights perspective. The CCLA acknowledged the central role played by the rape shield provisions in encouraging women to report rapes without fear that their own reputations would be up for scrutiny; but, the organization remained worried that the three exceptions to the rape shield rule, which were currently permitted, did not provide a wide enough net to catch men unjustly accused. It proposed, therefore, a broadening of these exceptions without jettisoning the entire rape shield provision.[36] As counsel for the Association Louise Arbour argued, "a wrongful conviction is not a fair price to pay for the benefits of encouraging women to come forward and testify."[37] The price women as a group pay when rapes go unreported is not calculated as part of the equation, the group perspective being one that stands outside the civil libertarian perspective.

When LEAF moved into the arena of issues involving violence against women, its tactic was to expose the male bias of current legal thinking. In doing so, it necessarily offered a group-based perspective that clashed fundamentally with individual rights. This was, of course, also evident in cases not involving violence against women, such as those discussed in chapter three. The group-based perspective in violence cases appeared more like a frontal assault than it did in other cases because cases involving violence against women illuminated a stark gender hierarchy – the man as rapist, the woman as victim. Neither men nor women enjoy identifying with these roles.

Women's daily reality as potential victims of sexual assault surfaced in another LEAF case where women's rights as a group were seen to conflict with the individual rights and freedoms of others. In October 1983, a man from Thunder Bay raped his wife using a weapon as a threat. At his trial a few months later, his wife applied to the court for a publication ban on his name, which was also her own, appealing to Section 442(3) of the Criminal

Code, which restricted the publication of facts disclosing the victim's identity in sexual assault cases where the victim or the prosecutor requested the
order, or where the court considered it necessary. The ban on publishing
the victim's name did not extend to publication of other facts of the case.
Canadian Newspapers, a major newspaper conglomerate, vigorously
opposed the use of Section 442(3) in the interests of freedom of the press. It
wanted the publication ban to be left up to the discretion of the judge in
each individual case.

As the case wound its way through the legal system, going all the way to
the Supreme Court of Canada and attracting along the way interventions
from LEAF and from the Canadian Civil Liberties Association, it became
obvious that certain assumptions about women and rape, related to the
ones at issue in *Seaboyer/ Gayme*, were at play. The original trial judge,
The Honourable Mr Justice Osbourne of the Supreme Court of Ontario,
endorsed a victim's right to control publication of her name noting the law's
purpose to encourage the reporting of sexual assaults. On appeal, however,
The Honourable Mr Justice Howland of the Court of Appeal, while
acknowledging the importance of the social value of reporting rapes, felt
that the victim's control of publication might have the impact of hindering
justice in some instances. For example, he hypothesized, a complainant
might be falsely accusing an accused and publication of her name could
bring forth witnesses to testify on his behalf. Here again the figure animat-
ing the legal approach was the vengeful woman described above by Susan
Estrich. It was an image powerful enough to prompt the Court of Appeal to
quash Section 442(3).

The importance given to the possibility of a vengeful woman was
underlined by the attention given to, and the controversy surrounding, the
testimony of Doreen Carole Boucher, the co-ordinator of a rape crisis centre. In cross-examination, Boucher was asked to comment on cases where a
man might be falsely accused of rape. When she acknowledged that such
cases existed, the lawyer cross-examining her characterized such occasions
as cases where an alleged victim wanted to humiliate a person. Although
Boucher explicitly stated that she did not know whether the intention in
such cases was to humiliate and that, in any event, such cases were
extremely rare, Mr Justice Howland predicated his decision on Boucher's
testimony as the lawyer had characterized it, completely ignoring the data

presented by the Attorney General of Canada on how threat of publication influenced a victim's decision to report a sexual assault.[38]

By the time the case came to the Supreme Court of Canada, Canadian Newspapers, recognizing Mr Justice Howland's misinterpretation of Boucher's testimony and fearing perhaps that this would constitute the basis for a reversal of the decision, focused almost entirely on Boucher's testimony, arguing that it constituted only "a minimal record" and did not address the justification of Section 442(3) as a reasonable limit on freedom of speech. In effect, Canadian Newspapers wanted the court to look elsewhere when it began the process of balancing competing claims. Elsewhere, in its view, was outside of Canada where other jurisdictions such as the United States endorsed the primacy of the right to freedom of speech.[39] In his article in *Chatelaine,* Michael Grieve, managing editor of Thunder Bay's *The Chronicle Herald,* the newspaper that sponsored the court challenge, rhapsodized about free and responsible reporting:

> Society's freedoms must not be compromised by misplaced fears. Secret trials must not be allowed, nor unacceptable social practices shielded from view. Ban the media from freely covering public courtrooms, and we are back in the 17th century.[40]

If a rape victim's fears surrounding the publication of her name were misplaced, if the image of the vengeful woman lay behind opposition to Section 442(3), and if the dispute remained in the eyes of many as one about freedom of speech, LEAF's role in the proceedings was obvious: return the focus to the victim of sexual assault, to the reality of violence against women. It approached this task in consultation with seven women's groups and organizations who had expertise in sexual assault and in feminist publishing.[41]

LEAF's approach in *Canadian Newspapers* took as its point of departure women's inequality, the same group-based perspective adopted in its other cases but refined here to accommodate the sordidness of women's reality as potential and actual victims of sexual assault. The factum submitted made explicit that LEAF's primary concern centred around the real conditions of women's lives, "the practical conditions under which victims of sexual assault, overwhelmingly women and children, must rely on government equally to protect and vindicate their legal rights – hence the social conditions under which all women and children, the primary target groups for sexual assault, can live on a daily basis."[42]

A "real-life" perspective began with the fact that it was men who sexually assaulted women. As it argued in *Seaboyer*, LEAF maintained that the gender dimensions of the crime indicated that rape was both "an indication and a practice of inequality between the sexes, specifically of the low status of women relative to men."[43] Sexual violence was described as a social practice, as opposed to an aberration, and its symbiotic link to women's inequality meant that "for a woman to be known as a victim of sexual assault is always stigmatic, frequently humiliating, and sometimes dangerous." LEAF expanded on this reality, noting that victims of sexual assault often experienced "rejection by family members, ostracism from the community, deteriorated work relationships, termination of employment, further terrorization, harassment, assault and silencing."[44] If victims could not exercise some control over the publication of the assault, they would be justifiably unwilling to report the crime. Unreported rapists exposed other women to risk. Addressing the issue of the vengeful woman, LEAF noted that allowing media and judicial control over what could be published "reveals a false assumption that certain women are knowably likely to be fabricating rape charges under certain factual conditions," a situation that, in any event, should be dealt with at trial, and not prior to it.[45]

The group-based view, the notion that all women need "to share the sense that they can expect equality of treatment and respect as well," led LEAF to make the argument under Section 15(2) of the Charter which allowed measures of positive discrimination in order to alleviate disadvantage. Such measures sheltered women from "specious equality-based attacks." Women needed special protection because they were disadvantaged relative to men – "economically, socially, politically, as targets for physical and sexual violence, and in access to credibility and expression." Section 442(3) of the Criminal Code explicitly recognized their reality and could be justified as an equality measure intended to alleviate disadvantage.[46]

From an argument for special measures, LEAF then turned to the argument of women's right to security of the person. If Section 442(3) were not in effect, many rapes would go unreported, leaving women exposed to further threat of rape. They would lose their "psychic freedom," suffer "serious state-imposed psychological stress," and an impaired freedom of movement. [47] (LEAF would later use this security of the person approach to challenge the actions of the police who knew the practices of a rapist but who, in the interests of catching him, failed to warn women in the neighbourhood of the potential threat to their person.)[48] Elaborating on what women's lives were like given that they could not count on security of the person, LEAF noted that women often avoided events or places where they might be at risk. It added: "Threat of sexual assault is threat of punishment for being female. Men, who are not subjected to the constant threat of rape and other forms of sexual assault as women are, have correspondingly greater security of the person, sense of security, and liberty of movement in society."[49]

That men and women have a different and unequal reality that must be explained in a court of law was clearly the underlying rationale of LEAF's submissions to the court. In one sense, such submissions were made with a great deal of optimism. If men knew what it was like to be female, they would see the need for laws such as 442(3). Certainly, many men have not personally confronted what the daily threat of rape to women implies. Lynn Smith recounted that one of her male colleagues once told her how much he liked to walk at sunset in a beautiful but isolated area. When she pointed out that she, too, shared his enjoyment of the area but could never hope to enjoy it as he did because several rapes had occurred there, he suddenly realized what lack of security of the person meant for women. [50] There was much more at issue in rape cases than a lack of information about women's reality, however. When LEAF identified women's daily reality, it could not do so without comparing women's group status with men's, thereby placing all men in positions of power. The focus in violence cases was not only on the inequality of the sexes, although this was disturbing enough, but on the life and death implications for women within this hierarchy. It was not a pretty picture.

One can only speculate on the full impact of LEAF's submissions on the Supreme Court of Canada in *Canadian Newspapers* since the final decision written by The Honourable Mr Justice Lamer did not address sex equality issues or elaborate on the security of the person arguments LEAF presented.

The court did, however, find sufficient justification to keep Section 442(3), basing its decision on the fact that if victims did not know in advance that publicity of their names would be definitely under their control, they would be less likely to report sexual assaults. In response to the concern that exceptions to the rape shield provisions are not sufficiently broad to protect the wrongfully accused, Mr Justice Lamer stated firmly that he considered this an issue of the right to a fair trial and that it was not under discussion in the present case; unfortunately for LEAF and Canadian women, the impact of the rape shield provisions on an accused's right to a fair trail could then become their next challenge in court.

In spite of the unpleasant realities of gender relations illuminated when women go to court to present aspects of the violence of their daily lives, there is some evidence that courts are, in fact, beginning to acknowledge the connections between violence against women and the power imbalances between the sexes. Take for example, in addition to the cases of sexual harassment and rape discussed above, the case of the balcony rapist, officially known as *Jane Doe v. Metropolitan Toronto Police.*

In February 1989 LEAF assisted a woman, who had been raped by the balcony rapist, in filing a suit for negligence against the police for failing to adequately warn women in the area about this serial rapist even though they possessed detailed information about his habits. At the hearing to determine whether or not the case would proceed to trial, the presiding judge expressed some confusion as to how women could be considered similarly situated to men, a relevant concept, in his view, given that LEAF was presenting police negligence as an issue of sex equality and security of the person. During the course of the hearing the *Andrews* decision was handed down. When LEAF counsel made the decision available, the judge decided that since the concept of similar situation had been discredited he would consider anew LEAF's arguments about what constituted a purposive approach to equality and granted permission for the suit to proceed to trial (both the negligence component under Section 7, security of the person, and the sex equality component under Sections 15 and 28, equality rights Charter challenge). This was a victory for LEAF and for women claiming their right to fight in court for full protection from rape.[51] In this instance, the dispensing of an old legal rule and the weight of evidence about the police's failure to adequately warn women clearly set the stage for a feminist use of the courts, that is for the protection of women and for the advancement of their rights. On February 5, 1991, *The Gazette* stated that the Ontario Court of Appeal made a unanimous decision to deny the police the right to appeal – a ruling that suggests judicial support for LEAF's arguments in this context.

Reproductive Issues: The Irreconcilable Sex Difference?

In a neat reversal of Freud's popular epigram, Mary O'Brien declares in *The Politics of Reproduction* that "men are necessarily rooted in biology, and their physiology is their fate."[52] That fate is alienation, the loss of connection to the race which is sustained by women through their capacity to reproduce. Men, in O'Brien's view, are condemned to resist such alienation, and their efforts have brought us such treasures as dualism, scientific discourse, and the like. They have sought, in short, to control women and nature, the only continuity and resistance to alienation they can establish. One need not accept O'Brien's thesis in its entirety to appreciate the kernel of truth about gender relations embedded in it (namely, that women's and men's different relationship to reproduction is the irreducible sex difference) and to see the obvious interconnectedness between the separation of the public and private, the rules of scientific discourse and the oppression of women by men. The cases of *Baby R.*, involving the legal apprehension of a foetus, and of *Borowski* concerning women's rights to abortion, illustrate these connections.

On May 20, 1987, the mother of the soon-to-be-born Baby R. checked into a Vancouver hospital. The events that unfolded over the next eight hours had the plot of a scarcely credible movie. The mother's labour was complicated, and the obstetrician on duty advised her to have a Caesarean section. When the mother declined, the obstetrician, who knew of her status as a woman on welfare, called the Family and Child Services Department seeking a legal way to apprehend the foetus and, if necessary, force the mother to undergo surgery. Remarkably, at 7:30 p.m., he contacted Mr Bulic, an official of that agency, who, within two hours, confirmed that the Superintendent of Child Welfare was apprehending the foetus. Shortly after, Bulic himself arrived at the hospital accompanied by staff and officers of the police emergency response team – all of whom intended to assist in apprehending the foetus from a pregnant woman in full labour. As it happened, the mother consented to the Caesarean at the last minute but was not told that her child had been seized until after her operation, whereupon Family and Child Services took Baby R. into its custody. [53] Several months later, The Honourable Mr Justice B.K. Davis of the Provincial Court of British Columbia had before him the case of *Baby R*. He ruled that the apprehension of the unborn child had been proper since the child had been in need of protection and further recommended that the infant continue to be kept in custody. [54]

Feminists were aghast at the implications of the apprehension of Baby R. prior to his birth. Initially, however, many expressed concern for the baby's welfare since Mr Justice Davis had based his decision on his opinion that, according to the testimony of the social workers who had evaluated her several years earlier, Baby R.'s mother was incapable of mothering. She was said to have used drugs and alcohol, to have been unable to organize her life sufficiently to keep appointments with social workers, and to have exhibited limited parenting skills. Her four previous children had also been seized, and this past history combined with her failure to judge what was in her child's best interests justified the apprehension. LEAF became involved in the case, in Lynn Smith's view, in spite of what seemed to be public sympathy, even among feminists, for the baby rather than the mother. By the time LEAF appeared as intervenor in the Supreme Court of British Columbia, however, the tide had shifted somewhat with many feminists beginning to see that lying beneath the official reports on her mothering was a woman maligned by social workers and in need of their support. [55]

LEAF's role in *Baby R*. was to make the connection between the apprehension of a foetus and infringements upon a pregnant woman's liberty and security of her person. *Baby R*. was, as Lynn Smith put it, a classic case of an individual's liberty, one that "falls squarely within anybody's agenda if they understand liberty as applying equally between men and women." [56] LEAF thus argued in its affidavit to the court on the basis of individual rights. Apprehension of a foetus necessarily entailed apprehension of a pregnant woman; to apprehend a foetus was also to apprehend a mother. The mother thereby lost her individual right to liberty and to security of the person. LEAF further stressed that imposing medical procedures on a pregnant woman set a dangerous precedent that offended a pregnant woman's right to security of the person.[57] In his judgement, The Honourable Mr Justice MacDonell agreed that "for the apprehension of a child to be effective there must be a measure of control over the body of the mother."[58] He further ruled that continuing seizure of Baby R. based on his mother's anticipated behaviour and lifestyle was unwarranted. Significantly, Mr Justice MacDonell found support for his judgement in the Common Law and not in the Charter, as LEAF had directed him to do, thereby leaving the door open for yet another challenge of foetal rights versus maternal rights.

The issue of foetal rights versus maternal rights can be fought without reference to group rights. What is at issue is clearly an individual's right to security of the person. It should, therefore, pose few problems for a court *unless* one is able to isolate the foetus from the womb that sustains it and somehow ignore that its existence is within a specific female body. If the foetus can be analytically separated from the mother, the way is clear for a balancing of their respective rights. *Baby R.* became an issue precisely because the original parties – the obstetrician, the Family and Child Services Department, and the original trial judge – were all able to take this analytical leap and to land squarely on the side of the foetus, no doubt because of the mother's disadvantaged status. They all had on their side rights discourse, where the balancing of claims without regard to an individual's ties is viewed as legitimate. Yet, as LEAF showed, one could in fact manipulate this discourse so that the reality of interconnected lives can be made relevant to the rights claim. In *Baby R.*, Mr Justice MacDonell declined to take up the issue of such balancing. However, in the case Joe Borowski brought to the courts over women's rights to abortion, balancing the rights of two theoretically autonomous beings provided a framework for infringing upon women's individual rights and for control of reproduction.

Scientific discourse is easily drafted into service for the appropriation of women's bodies through law, a feature that has not escaped individuals opposed to abortion. As Rosalind Pollack Petchesky writes of the film *Silent Scream*, which allegedly recorded the pain a foetus experienced when it was being aborted, the foetus is depicted in all its "abstract individ-ualism, effacing the pregnant woman and the foetus' dependence on her" an image consistent with the Hobbesian view of the disconnected solitary individual. [59] The foetus thus becomes an independent being, a patient having rights equal to its mother's. Petchesky also points out that with recent medical technology the foetus can be objectified, gazed at through machines, and given an empirically provable and separate existence. The privileging to visual proof in scientific discourse facilitated the separation of foetus from mother. The problem for women then is the same as it has been in all of LEAF's cases. In Petchesky's words, women have to "recontex-tualize the foetus ... place it back into the uterus, and the uterus back into the woman's body and her body back into its social space." [60] LEAF, con-fronting a court challenge of women's right to reproductive choice launched by Joe Borowski, attempted to do just that.

Joseph Borowski had been fighting Section 251 of the Criminal Code, which permitted therapeutic abortion, for ten years by the time the case ended up in the Supreme Court of Canada on October 3rd and 4th 1988. Although the Supreme Court had already struck down the offending sec-tion on the basis that it limited women's rights to abortion, [61] thereby ren-dering Borowski's case moot, the court agreed to hear his submissions in recognition of the importance of the issue. LEAF sought intervenor status submitting an application announcing its intention to argue that if the court recognized the rights of the foetus, as Borowski hoped, the equality rights of women would be seriously abridged. Thirteen women's and labour organizations supported its application. [62] Bearing an uncanny resemblance to LEAF's application, including whole phrases, REAL women (Realistic, Equal, Active for Life), a group opposed to abortion rights, sub-mitted its application for intervenor status announcing its intention to argue that abortion interferes with a woman's "physical and psychic integ-rity." [63] It, too, declared that it enjoyed support from twelve anti-abortion and religious organizations.

Borowski's arguments rested entirely on his claim that the foetus, whom he always referred to as the "child en ventre sa mère," enjoyed a separate and independent existence. By calling on no fewer than fifteen medical witnesses, including experts in electronic foetal monitoring, he sought to establish "the individuality, the separateness and the uniqueness of the human qualities of the unborn child," a claim that extended to the proposition that mother and child are "separate, distinctly different ... connected only by a placenta which is an external organ *of the child.*"[64] Enjoying an independent existence, the foetus-cum-child had a right to life as guaranteed under Section 7 of the Charter. In the courtroom, Borowski attempted to rely on the visual by first introducing the film *Silent Scream* and second by presenting a seven-month old (dead) foetus as evidence, an action he eventually refrained from on the advice of his lawyer. Arguments on the basis of morality sufficed instead, and Borowski's lawyer Moris Shumiatcher declared passionately to the court, "I feel now I'm on the side of the angels."[65] Shumiatcher then described a day in the life of the foetus whom he also referred to as the "child en ventre sa mère" prompting The Honourable Mr Justice Sopinka to interject that while no one knew what that phrase meant, everyone knew what was in a mother's body when she was pregnant.[66]

LEAF began its written argument by going straight to the point: "We invite the court to take judicial notice that the foetus exists within the body of a woman."[67] Although it then went on to ask the court to disregard Borowski's claim on the basis that Section 251 had already been declared inoperative by the court, LEAF developed the context in which a foetus exists, noting that foetal rights inevitably affected women's rights and opened the way for others to control pregnant women. In court, Mary Eberts elaborated on the issue of control. Offering examples of cases where women had been treated as mere vessels for babies, she noted that the impact of presenting the issues as a conflict between foetal and maternal rights was to suggest its resolution by a neutral arbiter. Women, in this scenario, effectively lost control of their bodies. As Petchesky advises in her article, the only effective response to the decontextualization of scientific discourse is "to image the pregnant woman, not as an abstraction, but within her total framework of relationships, economic and health needs and desires."[68] To do so, Mary Eberts once again made the connection between women's inequality and the case in question. Personhood for women was an uphill battle, she reminded the court, and women still did not have their reproductive needs acknowledged and accommodated in society. In its factum, LEAF explained fully the relevance of the social context of sex inequality to women's rights to abortion:

> Women have been socially disadvantaged in controlling sexual access to their bodies because of social learning, lack of information, inadequate or unsafe contraceptive technology, social pressure, custom, poverty and enforced economic dependence, sexual force and ineffective enforcement of laws against sexual assault. As a result, they often do not control the conditions under which they become pregnant.... Men as a group are not comparably disempowered by their reproductive capacities and are not generally required by society to spend their lives caring for children to the comparative preclusion of other life pursuits. [69]

The Supreme Court delivered its decision on the *Borowski* case on March 9, 1989, offering elaborate justification for why it felt the case had to be declared moot. [70] We have little indication in this case how receptive the court was to LEAF's efforts to contextualize women. At the very least, the courts did not declare for foetal rights. The arguments made by Borowski, however, indicated how amenable legal discourse is to rights claims that oppress women. The show of force in the case of *Baby R.* was an indication of where such claims can lead. [71] Ultimately, the "denial of the womb" can have "deadly consequences," not only for women but for humanity. As Petchesky suggests, a child in this context is a product to be appropriated, engineered, and exterminated at will. [72]

Canadian women will, in all likelihood, find themselves in court once again defending their right to reproductive choice. [73] Borowski himself has declared "we're going to fill the jails with our bodies" [74] by acts of civil disobedience, and newspapers have recently run stories of anti-abortion protesters on trial for just that. [75] In cases involving reproduction, rights language will surely be the weapon of choice on the part of the anti-abortionists. Feminist method in court will continue to consist of asking the court to contextualize the balancing of rights claims, but, while the issue looms as one where women will find not a crack in law into which women's realities can be poured but a chasm of gender difference, the Supreme Court's decision in *Morgentaler,* a case involving a doctor's right to perform abortions, and the political energies of the pro-choice movement offer hope that it may be otherwise. The decision of Madam Justice Wilson in the *Morgen-taler* case suggests how women can effectively subvert rights discourse from within. The decision to have an abortion, she writes,

> is one that will have profound psychological, economic and social conse-quences for the pregnant woman.... It is a decision that deeply reflects the way the woman thinks about herself and her relationship to others and to society at large. It is not just a medical decision; it is a profound social and ethical one as well. Her response to it will be the response of the whole per-son.... It is probably impossible for a man to respond, even imaginatively, to such a dilemma not just because it is outside the realm of his personal expe-rience (although this is of course the case) but because he can relate to it only by objectifying it, thereby eliminating the subjective elements of the female psyche which are at the heart of the dilemma. [76]

When feminists go to court they boldly "file a procession of real women before the court's eyes." Their approach "materializes them [women] in not only their bodies but their jobs, families, school-work, health prob-lems, young age, poverty, race/ethnic identity and dreams of a better life." [77] LEAF's method has consisted essentially of this contextualization. We may not yet know its full impact, and to be sure there are always prob-lems conveying the variety and contradiction of women's lives when one is bound by the rules of empirical proof. But the victories have been greater than defeats and there is evidence that the court is paying heed. Among many things left unanswered, however, is the question of whether men's and women's biological and social differences, characterized by feminists as the differences between the powerful and the powerless, are in the end too deeply entrenched and too expressive of the dominant discourse to be shattered in a court of law. One things *is* clear, however, the courtroom can-not be the only arena for confrontation.

What Counts
As Winning?

THE TERM "civil rights," Alice Walker writes, "is a term of limitation. Even as it promises assurance of greater freedoms it narrows the area in which people might expect to find them."[1] Rights thinking on the whole, a way of looking at the world that begins from the position that human beings operate as autonomous and isolated individuals, is a profoundly limiting and masculinist perspective. It is a way of thinking that, through the dualisms of reason and desire, public and private, and individual and community, denies the realities of women's lives and, most critically, represses the domination of women by men. How successful have feminists in law been in challenging rights thinking and what have been the concrete gains for women?

The Litigator's View

One way to answer the question, "what counts as winning?"[2] is to tally up the wins and losses LEAF has had in court, although a tally might be inappropriate given that LEAF is still relatively young. However, as Lynn Smith remarked in an interview, what counts in litigation is "that the judge gives you an order at the end of the day," an order that accepts at least some of the arguments you have made in court.[3] Success is seldom categorical since decisions may come to the right conclusion for the wrong reasons, and it is the reasons themselves that will matter to precedent. Furthermore, the equality potential may be buried so deep within the judgement that it is not clear how it represents a gain.

From a litigator's perspective, however, LEAF has enjoyed several gains and few obvious losses. It has been granted intervenor status a number of times, evidence of the credibility it has established as an organization able to speak on behalf of women's interests. LEAF has successfully conveyed its position on the importance of the equality guarantees of the Charter, and Canadian courts appear to have accepted its arguments about the adverse impact of certain practices on women – for example, the apprehension of the foetus in the *Baby R.* case and the denial of the rape victim's right to control whether or not her name was published in the *Canadian Newspapers* case. In *Schachter*, the one case where LEAF has been able to call and cross-examine witnesses, the court clearly accepted LEAF's arguments about the potential impact on women of sharing their childbirth leave with men. The watershed came in the *Andrews* case, when the court paid heed to LEAF's argument for its own approach to the balancing of competing claims under the Charter and for the rejection of the concept of similar situation. Subsequent to *Andrews*, there have been two landmark decisions: *Brooks, Allen, Dixon* established with certainty that pregnancy discrimination was sex discrimination, and *Janzen/Govereau* made clear that sexual harassment was sex discrimination. In both decisions, the court signalled its understanding of the impact that women's unequal status has on their rights and opportunities. Remarkably, there has also been some progress in getting the court to see how violence against women is a sex equality issue, as the court showed in permitting the case of *Jane Doe v. Metropolitan Toronto Police* to go to trial.

It is more difficult to assess the outcome of a case when it leaves the legal realm and moves into the bureaucracy. In *OSSOMM*, LEAF's intervention appeared to have prompted a change in the regulations governing the political activity of military spouses, yet ways have been found to circumvent the central issue at hand by permitting military spouses to engage in political activities but restricting their meetings to private homes. In the *Beaudette/Harvath* cases of spouse-in-the-house regulations, the overall impact of LEAF appears to be less positive than its initial reception. These cases bear further examination here because they illustrate the role an organization like LEAF can play, and at the same time they indicate the limitations of the legal route to social change if that route is the only one being taken.

Women's groups, anti-poverty groups, and self-help groups had been lobbying for a change to the spouse-in-the-house regulations for several years before LEAF was asked to take up the issue. [4] Until then, there had been little progress. Even an effort to lay a human rights complaint had floundered, largely due to the difficulties of proving how a practice, equally applied to all welfare claimants, adversely affected women. Bureaucratic implementation of the regulations was clearly aimed at women, however, with investigators of possible breaches being asked to look for evidence (such as men's boots, tracks in the snow, etc.) that a man had slept over the night in a welfare recipient's home. Without the Charter it was difficult to challenge such regulations and to make a clear-cut case for adverse impact discrimination. LEAF's involvement, therefore, profited by having the benefit of the Charter and by being able to take court action. Almost a year after the court challenge had been set in motion, the Ontario government approached LEAF for an out-of-court settlement.

LEAF met with the Attorney General of Ontario in 1986, and it is here that one begins to see the complexities of legal change as social change. He expressed a willingness to alter the regulations (for which LEAF might take some credit), but the problem of an alternate regulatory scheme remained unresolved. The government wanted to ensure that women on welfare were not receiving additional financial support, a desire fuelled by the conviction that in any heterosexual relationship the man supports the woman and children economically. In this view, the appropriate benefit unit was the family and not the individual claimant. This not only endangered women's economic independence but also flew in the face of reality. As the government itself acknowledged, women often lived with men who did not, in fact, contribute to their economic support, a situation they referred to as the "louse-in-the-house" scenario. Such complications meant that there was no clear-cut policy alternative to satisfy LEAF's equality concerns, the government's concern for abusers of the system, and for women's need to live an independent economic life. Most of all, giving women the benefit of the doubt, and taking into account their need for economic independence would cost money and this, after extensive consultation with LEAF, became the bottom line. At a law conference in November 1988, Attorney General of Ontario Ian Scott told his audience that the recent modifications to the spouse-in-the-house rule, which were made in order to bring it into compliance with the Charter, had cost taxpayers $80 million. He added: "I've got to give consideration to cancelling the whole welfare program for those women. That way there won't be any discrimination because there won't be any benefit given."[5]

LEAF saw its role limited to legal analysis, at least insofar as cases such as spouse-in-the-house regulations were concerned. As Helena Orton, LEAF's litigation director and chief negotiator for spouse-in-the-house, commented:

> We have an analysis that changes the nature of the debate and pushes them forward in a way that they can relate. It's not radical in the sense that an advocacy group can say 'this is not fair and this is the way it should be.'[6]

Yet issues such as welfare regulations cannot be approached so narrowly, nor indeed can most others, and there is no line between legal activity and political action. To challenge the regulations is to challenge a way of thinking about women, the family, and welfare. The legal challenge is only the tip of the iceberg, but it may well be that crack in the system through which alternate values might seep. Moreover, to confront the contempt that would lead a politician to claim that the only response to a discriminatory situation affecting women was to remove the benefit itself rather than the discrimination, women would have to be organized politically. Neither a legal nor a political challenge can be sustained without regard to the alternate values one espouses or how to win recognition for them politically. In this sense, legal challenges that end up on the bureaucratic treadmill, as many do, cannot result in long-term gain unless there is a clearly articulated political vision and one that finds support in the feminist community.

Elizabeth Schneider, defending the use of rights discourse, has suggested some questions feminists might ask themselves as a guide to evaluating the direction of their rights-based activities:

> Does the use of legal struggle generally and rights discourse in particular help build a social movement? Does articulating a right advance political

organizing and assist in political education? Can a right be articulated in a way that is consistent with the politics of an issue or that helps redefine it? Does the transformation of political insight into legal argumentation capture the political visions that underlie the movement? Does the use of rights keep us in touch with or divert us from consideration of and struggle around the hard questions of political choice and strategy?[7]

LEAF is at that stage in its history when the hard questions of political choice and strategy can no longer be avoided. The tightrope LEAF has walked between the feminist and the legal world is largely illusory. Litigation on behalf of women has to be explicitly feminist political activity or else it risks producing few real changes in women's lives. Laws can either directly oppress women, writes Kathy Lahey, or they can operate "to mediate feminist strategies within legal frameworks that have been largely determined by the legacy of male privilege and subjectivity in law."[8] Women's law reform activities can easily lose their transformative potential in the face of patriarchy's flexibility and the ease with which that flexibility can co-opt feminist reform.

Some of LEAF's newer projects illustrate the dangers of litigation as feminist political activity when there is no sound structure to facilitate a co-ordinated feminist response to women's oppression in law. Since 1987, LEAF has been working in coalition with immigrant women's groups on a challenge to the overtime provisions in the Employment Standards Act. Regulations to this act specifically exempt domestic workers, mainly minority and immigrant women, from the protections other Canadian workers enjoy, namely, overtime pay after forty-four hours of work per week. In practice this has meant that domestic workers often work seventy hours a week at a rate below the minimum wage.[9] Their positions are extremely vulnerable because most of them hold temporary permits, and, until recently, they were unable to change their place of employment without facing the threat of deportation. Regulations that stipulate such lesser rights derive their sustenance from a number of assumptions about domestic work and about the women who usually perform it – assumptions that LEAF will have to confront in court. Clearly domestic workers are undervalued in spite of the fact that a wide cross-section of Canada's middle class relies on them for child care and assistance in the home. Indeed, when the Ontario government attempted to reform the regulations, so that part-time nannies, for example, might be able to calculate overtime, one of the biggest hurdles it faced was the possible destruction of informal babysitting arrangements upon which many families with two working parents rely.

It is not only the assumptions about the value of domestic work that give these regulations their credibility, but also the view that it is permissible to treat differently workers who are not Canadian born. Certainly there is a racist and class cast to the objections voiced by employers of foreign domestics who complain that "the pendulum has swung too far" in protecting them, or when they complain that *their* rights are in jeopardy when domestics walk out on the employment contracts they have signed. The regulations of 1988 stipulate that a domestic worker who wishes to change jobs must get the approval of the immigration department which, however, cannot refuse permission unless there is gross evidence of a breach of contract on the domestic's part. Some employers would prefer that domestics be locked into a two-year contract, an employment situation one cannot imagine being tolerated by any Canadian worker but which is advanced as a reasonable limitation on the rights of domestic workers.[10]

Challenging certain sexist, racist, and class assumptions that underlie the law's treatment of domestic workers will require the co-ordinated effort of a variety of feminist groups. A project such as the challenge to the federal government's regulations governing who is eligible for subsidies for language training for new immigrants, or the challenge to prison regulations in P4W, entails not only the unmasking of the ideology behind the law, but also the articulation of a feminist vision for change to counter the inevitable bureaucratic search for a workable (i.e., cost efficient) solution in practice. Feminists will need to supply a response to the question of alternate regulations and be prepared to substantiate their views. LEAF, aware that it cannot speak on their behalf, is working in coalition with immigrant and native women's communities in some of the newer challenges.[11] But supplying the hard answers in such cases will take LEAF along a path where it has to examine its own brand of feminism self-consciously, with an eye to its own white middle-class character, and thus, to the assumptions it makes about the daily realities of communities unlike itself.

One assumption about women's reality that has formed the bedrock on which the feminist project in law has rested is the notion that all women share a core of oppression. It has been the task of LEAF to describe and empirically validate this core of sex oppression for the court's benefit; therefore, the focus has been on sexism in its most "uncontaminated"[12] form. From this basis, it has only been possible to deal with race oppression, for instance, in an additive way. That is, domestic workers of colour are considered oppressed as women and as minority workers; sexism is seen as separate from racism. This analytical approach leads to a fundamental misunderstanding of the realities of women who experience their multiple oppressions simultaneously. A Black domestic worker or a Native woman in the prison system are both unlikely to experience their gender in the same way that the predominantly white women teachers of Ontario do. Similarly, sexual harassment or rape cases "complicated" by issues of racism will demand different descriptions of women's sexuality and men's abuse of it.

The need to use analytical models that are based on the indivisibility and simultaneity of oppressions is more than just theoretical quibbling. LEAF will be unable to present various women's realities in all their complexities if gender remains the prism through which all other oppression is viewed. In order to understand the realities of Native women in the prison system, for example, LEAF will have to move beyond grafting race and class on sex oppression. When Fran Sugar invites us to look beyond the list of oppressions that typify a Native woman in prison (woman, Native, poor, and uneducated), she is asking us to move beyond what those categories mean to us, which in turn calls for a self-consciousness about our own privilege and history. Locating the historical and contemporary meaning of gender in this instance is contextualizing at its best. Leaving a foster home at sixteen might indicate strength of character; refusing a cleaning job in prison because the supervisor does not treat Native prisoners with respect looks like resistance, not insubordination.[13]

The Historian's View

Women using the Charter in the 1980s to improve their lives have waged an uphill battle. As the sceptics had warned, the Charter has been a vehicle for the advantaged; women have had only minimal access to its protection. The results of a study of the first three years of Charter jurisprudence, done under the auspices of the Canadian Advisory Council on the Status of Women, revealed that of the approximately 600 court decisions involving Section 15, only 44 decisions, or 7%, involved sex equality. Moreover, only 7 cases were initiated by or on behalf of women. Section 15 cases have not been mainly about the equality concerns of the disadvantaged, they have dealt with charges such as drunk driving and the manufacture of pop cans.[14] To put these figures into perspective, however, it is necessary to recall that the Canadian Advisory Council study surveyed only the first three years of Charter jurisprudence, and LEAF's victories have been most evident between late 1988 and early 1989. *Andrews,* which many observers see as a watershed case, is potentially the dawn of a new era in equality jurisprudence. LEAF's short history is an indication of what can happen when women go to court as an organized group to defend their rights. What remains troubling is women's severely limited access to the courts and the correspondingly greater use of the Charter by those groups who are already advantaged in Canadian society.[15]

Should women go to court at all? is a question that feminists have not generally considered relevant to Canada in the 1980s since, by and large, feminist legal activities have been defensive. From a historical perspective, however, the question of a more proactive approach has to be considered if only because feminist legal activities consume a great amount of energy and resources. Michael Mandel, writing of the legalization of politics under the Charter, makes the argument that since the Charter "leaves the hoards of power and power itself untouched," women and others who use the courts as a route to change can only expect a lateral redistribution of resources from the limited available pool. Hence, nothing remarkable in the way of a change in the status of groups can be won through legal change. In Mandel's words,

> The point is that using the Charter to improve general living standards is something like printing money to improve incomes. If anybody wins, it is going to be at somebody else's expense. General living standards cannot be improved through purely redistributive means, unless what is redistributed is *power.*[16]

According to this way of thinking, rights-based activities are a zero-sum game, a competition for one pie. Therefore, one man's desire for paid parental leave is presented as a competition between men and women; if the man is to get leave, it must be at the woman's expense.[17] Certainly Charter activities, like equality activities on the whole, exert a force that negates transformation and keeps the focus on a fairer redistribution of resources. As Mandel sees it, litigation expressive of rights thinking detaches form from substance so that the overall picture, the transforming vision, gets lost in the shuffle. Feminists in the courtroom are primarily concerned with resisting this built-in feature of the discourse in which they work, insisting on transformation and on context. One can remain reasonably cautious about this work, recognizing its limitations, without coming to Mandel's conclusion that using the law as a route to social change is "a big mistake."[18]

There are, nonetheless, sound reasons for approaching the project of feminism applied to law with an ever watchful eye to its necessary links to a wider feminist vision for change. Women's success in the courts thus far has to be seen in the wider perspective of the values that predominate in Canadian society. Rights discourse is everywhere, and the historian concerned with feminist rights-based activities in the 1980s finds herself confronted with daily newspaper reports of social conflicts expressed in the language of rights. An article in *The Toronto Star*, for instance, describing a local men's group's intention to legally challenge the existence of women-only self-defence courses, notes that the group in question claims that men are more likely to be assaulted than women.[19] (The challenge to women's self-defence courses was soon taken up by LEAF.) The newsworthiness of the men's challenge lay in the curious inversion of an everyday reality using the familiar discourse of rights. Women's reality as victims of sexual assaults by men is equated with men's as victims of other kinds of assault, although the men's group did not specify what these were. Men, in the interest of the equal right to protection, had the right to take the self-defence classes. The inversion of reality fed on the premise that men and women enjoy equal opportunities and freedoms, that they are, in a word, equal. Carol Smart has pointed out the application of this aspect of rights-based thinking in matrimonial law: Law reform efforts of the 1980s encouraged by the image of the divorced woman as parasite, have tried in some jurisdictions to limit a man's financial obligations; men, therefore, become the victims, and the reality of women's economic status is ignored.[20]

Judges, Alan Hutchinson wrote, "cannot stem the tide of social change but must ride the historical surf."[21] The historical surf in 1980s Canada was one where the heritage of liberalism infused social views about rights and responsibilities. The premise that we are all autonomous individuals whose competing claims must be weighed as though we are equal still remains a widely accepted one. Inversions of reality are necessary to fit claims into this mould. For a variety of reasons, among them the tendency to ignore the real-life details surrounding rights claims, women and minorities often fail to have their particular situation acknowledged. The weighing of competing claims *in context* is a position resisted in many quarters.

Nowhere is the rights-based line of thinking more evident than in the claims of men's rights groups in the 1980s. Although an extremely small minority (estimates are that there are less than eighty activists across Canada),[22] such groups[23] have garnered more than their share of press and political attention, a testimony to the chords they strike in popular thinking. Their political agenda embodies the underlying premises of liberalism and of rights discourse, although they stretch liberalism to its limits in the intensity of their anti-woman positions. For instance, they strongly support mandatory joint custody arrangements and legal limits on the ability of either parent to opt out of the arrangement (through mandatory mediation, for example), a position that does not admit the very real power imbalances that invade family relationships. For many father's rights groups, the realities of child sexual abuse, battered women, and women who are economically and socially disadvantaged in comparison with men are realities that simply do not exist. The real child abuse, as these groups suggested at a recent conference, is women's sole custody of children.[24] An interviewer, canvassing the opinion of a men's rights activist Ross Virgin, revealed both the movement's extremism and its solid appeal to rights-based analysis. By 1991, Virgin wants, among other things, to have alimony and child support payments eliminated; by 1994, sexual abuse laws changed so that women cannot use the laws as "weapons" against men. Such changes, Virgin maintains, would give men and women equal rights and equal responsibilities.[25]

The myths that buttress a seemingly extremist fringe in Canadian society are powerful and widespread. As Susan Crean writes, at "the heart of the controversy over joint custody, access, mediation, and the other issues related to marriage breakup lies the concept of the family which is, ultimately, what is being fought over – or, more precisely, the place of male authority in the family."[26] Rights discourse, as LEAF as well as advantaged individuals and groups have found in court, is particularly well suited for expressing this ideal. In its insistence on each individual's essential autonomy, moreover, it eliminates the real life details that feminists insist upon, the naming of oppression that many men and women prefer to suppress.

The Feminist View

The project that is feminism applied to law is fundamentally a project of naming, of exposing the world as man-made. Men, Ann Scales writes, have had the power to organize reality, "to create the world from their own point of view, and then, by a truly remarkable philosophical conjure, were able to elevate that point of view into so-called 'objective reality'."[27] Women find themselves demystifying that reality and challenging its validity. In law, the issues that preoccupy women, Scales notes, are all issues that emerge out of a male-defined version of female sexuality. Abortion, contraception, sexual harassment, pornography, prostitution, rape, and incest are "struggles with our otherness," that is, struggles born out of the condition of being other than male.[28] One can add to Scales's characterization that law also sees minorities in the same way and that the issues that concern people of colour emerge out of white domination. Thus, when white women argue in court for context, it is from their own position of otherness that they speak. It is this exclusiveness of perspective that must be avoided at all costs.

The realities that feminists name in court force a showdown between the discourse that denies women's context and the oppression of women by men and the world view of feminism that is built upon the integrity and necessary integration of women's experiences, however diverse and historically constructed those are. What are the consequences of naming? As long as we keep in mind Denise Riley's caution about "the impermanence of collective identities," and "skate across the several identities which will take (our) weight,"[29] naming has a significant role to play in feminism. It can empower women and draw us together. Adrienne Rich sums this up eloquently:

> Women have been driven mad, 'gaslighted,' for centuries by the refutation of our experience and our instincts in a culture which validates only male experience. The truth of our bodies and our minds has been mystified to us. We therefore have a primary obligation to each other: not to undermine each others' sense of reality for the sake of expediency; not to gaslight each other.
>
> Women have often felt insane when cleaving to the truth of our experience. Our future depends on the sanity of each of us, and we have a profound stake, beyond the personal, in the project of describing our reality as candidly and fully as we can to each other.[30]

It may be that naming thrusts us into "formlessness,"[31] and it is certain that there will be resistance to what is named, but it also brings with it a profound relief that some of the realities we live as women will be finally brought to light. Feminism applied to law has an important role to play in this process.

❖

ABBREVIATIONS
OF COURTS CITED

ALTA. C.Q.B.	Alberta Court of Queen's Bench
B.C.C.A.	British Columbia Court of Appeal
B.C.P.C.	British Columbia Provincial Court
B.C.S.C.	British Columbia Supreme Court
C.A.S.C. ONT.	Court of Appeal, Supreme Court of Ontario
F.C.C.T.D.	Federal Court of Canada, Trial Division
MAN. C.A.	Manitoba Court of Appeal
S.C.C.	Supreme Court of Canada
S.C. ONT.	Supreme Court of Ontario
TORONTO WEEKLY COURT, S.C. ONT.	Toronto Weekly Court, Supreme Court of Ontario

NOTES

Introduction

A version of this chapter appeared as "Revolution From Within: Dilemmas of Feminist Jurisprudence," in *Queen's Quarterly* 97, 3 (Autumn 1990): 398-413.

1. Elizabeth Wolgast, "Wrong Rights," *Hypatia* 2, 1 (Winter 1987): 25.

2. In legal texts, Rawls is often cited as an authority and it is for this reason that it is primarily his version of the social contract that is addressed here. Rawls, as Mari Matsuda has pointed out, chooses abstraction as a methodology, a standard feature of liberal thinkers, and the main reason why liberal theories of justice, and rights thinking on the whole, fail to take into account the real oppression of women's lives. See Matsuda, "Liberal Jurisprudence and Abstracted Visions of Human Nature: A Feminist Critique of Rawls' Theory of Justice," *New Mexico Law Review* 16 (1986): 613.

3. Michael J. Sandel, *Liberalism and the Limits of Justice* (Cambridge: Cambridge University Press, 1982), 1.

4. Roberto Mangabiera Unger, *Knowledge and Politics* (New York: The Free Press, 1975), 6.

5. Ronald Dworkin, *Taking Rights Seriously* (Cambridge, Mass.: Harvard University Press, 1977), 227. Cited by Zillah Eisenstein in *The Female Body and the Law* (Minneapolis: University of Minnesota Press, 1988), 218-219.

6. John Rawls, *A Theory of Justice* (Cambridge: Harvard University Press, 1971), 76-90, and Matsuda, "Liberal Jurisprudence," 615.

7. Sandel, *Liberalism,* 176, 179.

8. Joseph Singer, "The Player and the Cards: Nihilism and Legal Theory," *Yale Law Journal* 94, 1 (November 1984): 30.

9. Naomi Scheman, "Individualism and the Objects of Psychology," Sandra Harding and Merrill Hintikka, eds., *Discovering Reality* (Holland: D. Reidel Publishing Co., 1983), 231.

10. *Ibid.,* 232.

11. Robin West, "Jurisprudence and Gender," *The University of Chicago Law Review* 55, 1 (Winter 1988): 42.

12. Larry May argues this, for example, when he suggests that an employer is liable for sexual harassment perpetrated by a male employee because that male employee derived his power to harass from an environment (maintained by the employer and society) where such harassment was, if not condoned, at least made possible. *The Morality of Groups* (Indiana: University of Notre Dame Press, 1987), 30.

13. Kenneth Karst, "Women's Constitution," *Duke Law Journal* 3 (June 1984): 467.

14. Joan Tronto, "Beyond Gender Difference To A Theory of Care," *Signs* 12, 4 (Summer 1987): 660.

15. Alice Jardine, *Gynesis. Configurations on Woman and Modernity* (Ithaca: Cornell University Press, 1985), 17.

16. Tronto, "Beyond Gender Difference," 660.

17. Karst, "A Woman's Constitution," 472.

18. Elizabeth Schneider, "The Dialectic of Rights and Politics: Perspectives from the Women's Movement," *New York University Law Review* 61 (October 1986): 599.

19. Robert A. Williams, "Taking Rights Aggressively: The Perils and Promise of Critical Legal Theory for Peoples of Color," *Law and Inequality* 5 (1987): 130.

20. May, *The Morality of Groups,* 136.

21. Leslie Armour, "Human Rights: A Canadian View," Alan S. Rosenbaum, ed., *The Philosophy of Human Rights* (Conn.: Greenwood Press, 1980), 47.

22. Catharine MacKinnon, *Sexual Harassment of Working Women* (New Haven: Yale University Press, 1979), 117.

23. Jill Vickers, "Equality Theories and Their Results: Equality-seeking in a Cold Climate," in Lynn Smith and Magda Seydegart, eds., *Righting The Balance* (Toronto: Carswell, 1987), 19.

24. Postmodernist and poststructuralist are terms used interchangeably in this text. They refer to an intellectual movement based largely in France during the 1970s. The movement included such writers as Jacques Lacan, Jacques Derrida, Michel Foucault, and Julia Kristeva. Two texts which have been relied on extensively in the following discussion are: Chris Weedon, *Feminist Practice and Poststructuralist Theory* (Oxford: Basil Blackwell, 1987), and Alice Jardine, *Gynesis. Configurations of Woman and Modernity.*

25. Jane Flax, "Postmodernism and Gender Relations in Feminist Theory," *Signs* 12, 4 (Summer 1987): 621.

26. Jean-François Lyotard, *The Post-Modern Condition: A Report on Knowledge,* translated from the French by Geoff Bennington and Brian Massumi (Minneapolis: University of Minnesota Press, 1986), xxiii.

27. Singer, "The Player and the Cards," 31.

28. Lyotard, *The Post-Modern Condition,* 34.

29. Eisenstein, *The Female Body and The Law,* 43.

30. Singer, "The Player and the Cards," 56.

31. Beverly Baines, "Women and the Law," in Sandra Burt *et al.,* eds., *Changing Patterns. Women in Canada* (Toronto: McClelland and Stewart, 1988), 158-170. Examples of such cases include Mabel Penery French in 1905 in New Brunswick and 1911 in British Columbia, and Annie MacDonald Langstaff in 1915 in Quebec, both of whom sued for the right to practice law.

32. *Ibid.,* 170.

33. There were approximately seven journals in North America by 1986, including the *Canadian Journal of Women and the Law.*

34. Wendy Williams, "The Equality Crisis: Some Reflections on Culture, Courts, and Feminism," *Women's Rights Law Reporter* 7, 3 (Spring 1982): 182.

35. Wendy Williams, "American Equality Jurisprudence," in Sheilah L. Martin and Kathleen Mahoney, eds., *Equality and Judicial Neutrality* (Toronto: Carswell, 1987), 123.

36. Ann C. Scales, "Toward A Feminist Jurisprudence," *Indiana Law Journal* 56, 3 (1980–81): 435.

37. Wolgast is referred to in the Charter of Rights Educational Fund, *Report of the Statute Audit Project* (Toronto, January, 1985), I.29.

38. Marie Ashe, "Mind's Opportunity: Birthing a Poststructuralist Feminist Jurisprudence," *Syracuse Law Review* 38 (1987): 1139.

39. Anne Simon, review of *The Politics of Law: A Progressive Critique,* edited by David Kairys, *Women's Rights Law Reporter* 8, 3 (Summer 1985): 199-204.

40. Janet Rifkin, "Toward a Theory of Law and Patriarchy," *Harvard Women's Law Journal* 3 (1980): 95.

41. Christine Littleton, "In Search of a Feminist Jurisprudence," *Harvard Women's Law Journal* 10 (1987): 6.

42. West, "Jurisprudence and Gender," 70.

43. Suzanna Sherry, "The Gender of Judges," *Law and Inequality* 4 (1986): 164.

44. Denise Riley, *"Am I That Name?" Feminism and the Category of 'Women' in History* (Minneapolis: University of Minnesota Press, 1988), 13.

45. Trinh T. Minh-ha, *Woman, Native, Other* (Bloomington and Indianapolis: Indiana University Press, 1989), 106.

46. Christine Boyle, "Sexual Assault and the Feminist Judge," *Canadian Journal of Women and the Law* 1 (1985): 103.

47. *Ibid.,* 105.

48. Christine Boyle, "A Feminist Approach to Criminal Defences," unpublished draft, July 1988, 14.

49. Shelley Gavigan, "Women, Law and Patriarchal Relations," in Neil Boyd, ed., *The Social Dimensions of Law* (Scarborough, Ontario: Prentice Hall, 1986), 103-105. Christine Boyle has also pointed out that rape as violence makes it difficult to include the rape of children who do not resist in ways that would indicate violence has occurred.

50. *Ibid.,* 107.

51. Mary O'Brien and Shiela McIntyre, "Patriarchal Hegemony and Legal Education," *Canadian Journal of Women and the Law* 2 (1986): 70.

Chapter One

1. Cerise Morris, "Determination and Thoroughness: The Movement for a Royal Commission on the Status of Women in Canada," *Atlantis* 5, No. 2 (Spring 1980): 1.

2. Florence Bird, *Report of the Royal Commission on the Status of Women* (Ottawa: Queen's Printer, 1970), xi.

3. *Ibid.*

4. Jill Vickers, "Major Equality Issues of the Eighties," in Jean-Denis Archambeault and R. Paul Nadin-Davis, eds., *Canadian Human Rights Yearbook 1983* (Toronto: Carswell, 1983), 56.

5. William Black, "From Intent to Effect," *Canadian Human Rights Reporter* (February, 1980): chapter 1.

6. *Ibid.*, chapter 3.

7. For an account of this period see Mary Eberts, "Women and Constitutional Renewal," in Audrey Doerr and Micheline Carrier, eds., *Women and the Constitution of Canada* (Ottawa: Ministry of Supply and Services, 1981), 3-27.

8. Eberts, "Women and Constitutional Renewal," 5. Eberts does not mention that the issue of constitutional change was a highly contentious one within NAC that resulted in Quebec groups breaking away from NAC.

9. Beverly Baines, "Women, Human Rights and the Constitution," paper prepared for the CACSW, Ottawa, August 1980 and revised October, 1980, in *Women and the Constitution of Canada*, 31-63.

10. *Ibid.*, 33.

11. Lynn Smith, "A New Paradigm for Equality Rights," in *Righting the Balance*, 375.

12. Baines, "Women, Human Rights and the Constitution," 43.

13. *Ibid.*, 51.

14. Vickers, "Major Equality Issues," 64.

15. Baines, "Women, Human Rights and the Constitution," 58.

16. Marc Emmett Gold, "Equality Before the Law in the Supreme Court of Canada: A Case Study," *Osgoode Hall Law Journal* 18, 3 (1980): 383.

17. Rosemary Billings in *The Taking of Twenty-Eight*, Penney Kome (Toronto: The Women's Press, 1983), 17.

18. *Ibid.*

19. Myra Marx Ferree and Beth B. Hess used this term to refer to the development of a women's lobby in the U.S. in *Controversy and Coalition* (Boston: Twayne Publishers, 1985), 117.

20. Christine Appelle, "The New Parliament of Women: A study of the National Action Committee on the Status of Women," M.A. thesis, Carlton University, 1987, chapter 4.

21. Interview with Linda Ryan-Nye by Penney Kome. Tape recordings in personal files of Penney Kome.

22. In Toronto on March 21, 1988, I chaired a round table discussion with Beth Atcheson, Denise Arsenault, Marilou McPhedran, and Beth Symes on the founding of LEAF, tape recording, LEAF national office. Subsequently referred to as the round table discussion.

23. Constitution Act, 1982 [en. by the Canada Act 1982 (U.K.), c. 11, s. 1], pt. I (Canadian Charter of Rights and Freedoms).

24. Vickers, "Major Equality Issues, 62.

25. Reported by Rosemary Billings in *The Taking of Twenty-Eight*, 18.

26. Marilou McPhedran's diary in her possession, entry for March 13, 1981.

27. Round table discussion.

28. Round table discussion.

29. Beth Atcheson, round table discussion.

30. Bob Bettson, "Women's Clause Unneeded," *Calgary Herald*, January 29, 1982.

31. Round table discussion.

32. Round table discussion.

33. Beth Atcheson in a letter to Magda Seydegart, July 28, 1982 re: the purpose of the symposium. Personal Files of Magda Seydegart.

34. Minutes of CREF, January 15, 1983, Nancy Jackman files.

35. Minutes of CREF, February 2, 1983, Nancy Jackman files. The number who attended the second meeting is not known.

36. Beth Atcheson, "Section 15, Equality Rights," in Charter of Rights Educational Fund, in *The Study Day Papers* (Toronto, 1983): 2.6.

37. Katherine Swinton, "Introduction to the Charter," in *The Study Day Papers*, 1.8.

38. Marilou McPhedran, "Section 28. Was it Worth the Fight?" in *The Study Day Papers*, 4.4.

39. Round table discussion.

40. Charter of Rights Educational Fund, *Report of the Statute Audit Project*, 1.24.

41. *Ibid.*, 1.28-1.29.

42. CORC document in educational kit, Nancy Jackman files.

43. Nancy Jackman feels that with the exception of BC., CORC women did not ultimately become LEAF women. Interview with author, Toronto, March 11, 1988, tape

recording, LEAF national office. The participants of the round tale discussion recalled, however, that the cross-country speaking they did, while on other business, either for *Women and Legal Action* or for CORC, facilitated organizing support for a litigation fund.

44. Nancy Jackman, interview with author, Toronto, March 11, 1988, tape recording, LEAF national office.

45. Anne Bayevsky and Mary Eberts, eds., *Equality Rights and the Canadian Charter of Rights and Freedoms* (Toronto: Carswell, 1985).

46. Julianne Labreche, "Women's Pressure Groups. What's Their Role in the 1980's?", *Chatelaine* (July, 1982): 78.

47. Dianne L. Martin, "Symposium Reveals Tension Between Law and Justice," *Lawyers Weekly* 4, 14 (February 15, 1985): 6.

48. Marilou McPhedran, Notes for the Charter workshop, May 22, 23, 1982, in author's possession.

49. *Ibid.*

50. Mary Eberts, interview with the author, Toronto, April 28, 1988, tape recording, LEAF national office.

51. Round table discussion.

52. McPhedran, interview with author, Toronto, June 2, 1988, tape recording, LEAF national office.

53. Nancy Jackman, interview with author, Toronto, March 11, 1988, tape recording, LEAF national office.

54. This is the way Magda Seydegart expressed her role in co-editing *Righting the Balance,* the book that came out of the symposium on equality rights.

55. Magda Seydegart, interview with the author, Toronto, March 30, 1988, tape recording, LEAF national office.

56. Marilou McPhedran, interview with the author, Toronto, June 9, 1988, tape recording, LEAF national office.

57. Beth Atcheson, round table discussion.

58. Beth Atcheson, round table discussion. Unless otherwise indicated, all subsequent references to Beth Atcheson are from the round table discussion.

59. Minutes of LEAF, August 9, 1984, Magda Seydegart's files.

60. Minutes of LEAF, September 5, 1984, Magda Seydegart's files.

61. Minutes of LEAF, Novermber 9, 1984, Magda Seydegart's files.

62. Magda Seydegart, interview with the author, Toronto, March 30, 1988, tape recording, LEAF national office.

63. Shelagh Day became LEAF's first director, Gwen Brodsky its first litigation director. The first legal committee included: Mary Eberts, Lynn Smith, Beth Symes, Dale Gibson, Daphne Dumont, and Jenny Abell. The board of directors included a chair (Susan Tanner); a vice-chair (Beth Atcheson); a legal chair (Mary Eberts); a finance chair (Denise Arsenault); a fundraising chair (Nancy Jackman); a public education and research chair (Shauna MacKenzie); a chair of governmental relations (Magda Seydegart); and representatives in each region of Canada. *Leaf Litigation Year One*, a report by Mary Eberts and Gwen Brodsky, March 31, 1986.

64. Mary Eberts, "A Strategy for Equality Litigation Under the Canadian Charter of Rights and Freedoms," in Joseph M. Neiler and Robin M. Elliot, eds., *Litigating the Values of a Nation: The Canadian Charter of Rights and Freedoms* (Toronto: Carswell, 1986), 417.

65. Round table discussion.

66. Round table discussion.

67. O'Malley v. Simpsons-Sears, *Canadian Human Rights Reporter* 7 (1985): D3102.

68. Lynn Smith, "A New Paradigm for Equality Rights," 354.

69. Magda Seydegart noted in an interview with the author, Toronto, March 30, 1988, that she felt there was a whole linguistic revolution in the human rights field from "target groups" to "equality seekers."

70. Lynn Smith, "A New Paradigm For Equality Rights," 375.

71. Magda Seydegart, Notes made to the text of her interview, April 5, 1988.

72. Vickers, "Equality-Theories and Their Results," 12.

Chapter Two

1. Beth Atcheson, round table discussion.

2. Karen O'Connor described three approaches to litigation as political action: outcome-oriented litigation involving test cases designed to build precedent incrementally (such as is pursued by the NAACP); *amicus curiae* or friend of the court interventions where the objective is usually to ensure that a particular argument is heard or to provide new non-legal data; publicity-oriented litigation where

there might be little hope of winning but the intent is to publicize an issue or gain credibility, in *Women's Organizations' Use of the Courts* (Mass.: Lexington Books, 1980), 3-5. In the last two instances, one must be able to demonstrate to the court sufficient cause to be granted intervenor status. Courts, faced with ever-increasing caseloads, are typically reluctant to grant intervenor status and even less willing to expand the issues which the intervenor is entitled to address. Only rarely are intervenors allowed to bring evidence, cross-examine, etc.

3. Karen O'Connor, *Women's Organizations'*, 18-28.

4. Mary Eberts, interview with the author, Toronto, April 26, 1988, tape recording, LEAF national office.

5. *Leaf Litigation Year One*, Report by Mary Eberts and Gwen Brodsky, March 31, 1986, 2.

6. In a flyer signed by Marilou McPhedran, sample legal costs for one of LEAF's cases are given as follows: "Direct costs (bring in expert witnesses, telephone bills, photocopying of legal documents, lawyers fees at the legal aid rate, etc.) amounted to $55,000. Unlike most of our cases, a little over half ($35,000) was funded by the Canadian Court Challenges program. Normally we must fundraise all the money to pay these costs. Indirect costs, such as the time spent on staff support of the volunteers, can be estimated at $10,000. That means that LEAF has to fundraise at least $30,000. And this is only one of the 60 cases LEAF has sponsored on behalf of Canadian women." Legal Education and Action Fund, *Equality '89* Flyer.

7. On October 16, 1985, the Ontario government offered LEAF a fund of one million dollars to finance equality litigation for Ontario women. The fund must be used specifically to defray legal costs. LEAF receives approximately 50% of its budget from government sources such as the Ontario fund and from the federal government's Charter fund adminstered by the Canadian Council on Social Development. However, only one-third of government funding is "core funding," that is money which LEAF can more or less depend upon for operational costs, etc. The remainder has to be applied for on a case-by-case basis. Thus in 1988, for example, LEAF had to raise $200,000 to cover the costs of cases currently in progress. This information comes from Christie Jefferson, LEAF's executive director, in an interview with the author May 11, 1988.

8. Marilou McPhedran, round table discussion.

9. Beth Atcheson, round table discussion.

10. This was true of the roster of LEAF volunteers as well as the small paid staff. However, as Mary Eberts noted in an interview, paid staff differ in one significant respect from volunteers in that the former do not operate in the highly paid corporate legal environment that many of LEAF's volunteer women do.

11. Andrea Nye, "Women Clothed With the Sun: Julia Kristeva and the Escape From/To Language," *Signs* 12, 4 (Summer, 1987): 671.

12. Pat Wouters, LEAF board member, interview with the author, Toronto, February 19, 1988, tape recording, LEAF national office.

13. Magda Seydegart, in notes to an interview, March 30, 1988, referring to the task-oriented as opposed to process-oriented mode of LEAF at the time of her involvement.

14. Mary Eberts, interview with the author, Toronto, April 26, 1988, tape recording, LEAF national office.

15. *Seaboyer/Gayme v. Her Majesty the Queen* [1985] Judgment – 22 November 1985, Gilligan J. (TORONTO WEEKLY COURT, S.C. ONT.). The Supreme Court ruling on this case is still not yet released (November 1990).

16. Factum on Behalf of the Intervenant, the Women's Legal Education and Action Fund, *Seaboyer/Gayme v. Her Majesty the Queen*, Court File No. 985/85 and 986/85, n.d. (C.A.S.C. ONT.).

17. Ironically, the Court of Appeal accepted LEAF's arguments.

18. Information on LEAF's experience with *Seaboyer/Gayme* comes from interviews by the author with Christie Jefferson, LEAF's executive director, Toronto, March 1 and 11, 1988, and Mary Eberts, Toronto, April 28, 1988, tape recordings, LEAF national office.

19. Legal Education and Action Fund, *Litigation Works. A Report on LEAF Litigation YEAR TWO* (Toronto: Carswell, 1987), 4.

20. Memo submitted by Carmencita R. Hernandez, Vice-President, Ontario Region, National Organization of Immigrant and Visible Minority Women of Canada, Toronto, November 6, 1987. Christie Jefferson's Files.

21. Nancy Jackman in an interview with the author, Toronto, March 11, 1988, tape recording, LEAF national office.

22. Mary Eberts, interview with the author, Toronto, April 26, 1988.

23. Susan Cole reported in *Broadside*, November 1987, that some feminists in the community even began to consider Meech Lake a "make-work project for professional feminists." Further, the Ontario region of the National Organization of Immigrant and Visible Minority Women of Canada condemned LEAF's views on the Meech Lake Accord as focusing mainly on rights for English-speaking Canadians. (Minutes of the meeting of November 6, 1987, recorded by Carmencita Hernandez and sent to LEAF.)

24. Deborah Wilson, "Ruling on Nanny Tax Break Assailed as Benefit to the Rich," *The Globe and Mail*, May 17, 1989, A12.

25. Richard Kluger, *Simple Justice* (New York: Vintage Books, 1977), 749.

26. Schneider, "Dialectic," 599.

27. Margaret Berger, *Litigation on Behalf of Women. A Review for the Ford Foundation* (New York: The Ford Foundation, 1980), 16. *Griggs v. Duke Power* was decided in 1971. The case concerned requirements that applicants for the position of janitor in a school possess a high school diploma and pass an intelligence test. Both requirements effectively screened out Black applicants for the job and the court ruled that no intent was necessary to consider these requirements discriminatory.

28. R. v. Big M Drug Mart Ltd., *Western Weekly Reports* 3, (1985): 524.

29. *Ibid.*, 527.

30. Beatrice Vizkelety, *Proving Discrimination in Canada* (Toronto: Carswell, 1987), 3.

31. R. v. Oakes, *Supreme Court Review* 1 (1986): 103.

32. Mary Eberts, "Risks of Equality Litigation," in *Equality and Judicial Neutrality,* 101.

33. Beth Symes, round table discussion.

34. Attributed to Wendy Williams by Elizabeth Schneider, moderator, "Lesbians, Gays and Feminists at the Bar: Translating Effective Legal Argument – A Symposium," *Women's Rights Law Reporter* 10, 3 (Winter 1988): 121.

35. These figures come from LEAF's research officer Susan Joannis, February 27, 1989.

36. LEAF, *Litigation Works,* 3.

37. Carol Smart, "'There is of course the distinction dictated by nature': Law and the Problem of Paternity," in Michelle Stanworth, ed., *Reproductive Technologies. Gender, Motherhood and Medicine* (Minneapolis: University of Minnesota Press, 1987), 111.

38. Eberts and Brodsky, *Leaf Litigation Year One,* 3.

39. LEAF, *Litigation Works,* 6.

40. Eberts and Brodsky, *Leaf Litigation Year One,* 4.

41. *Ibid.*, 4.

42. Rick Haliechuk, "Women's Class Discriminatory, Men's Group Complaint Says," *The Toronto Star*, February 16, 1988.

43. Michael Mandel, *The Charter of Rights and the Legalization of Politics in Canada* (Toronto: Wall and Thompson Inc., 1989), 270. In Mandel's view, the case of Justine Blainey represented a symbolic victory for women at the expense of the rights of women involved in women-only teams.

44. See my Conclusion for an evaluation of the result of lengthy committee work in this case.

45. It was rumoured that the Law Society's sudden interest in this issue developed when it faced what it considered to be an influx of lawyers trained in Hong Kong who, as British subjects, were entitled to practice law in Canada. The racist cast of the Society's sudden urge to defend its rule of citizenship was taken up in LEAF's submissions to the court. Mary Eberts, Presentation on the Andrews case in the Department of History and Philosophy, the Ontario Institute for Studies in Education, Toronto, April 12, 1989.

46. LEAF helped the *La Maison des Femmes de La Côte-Nord* a woman's shelter in the trial of the murder of its co-ordinator by her husband and helped battered women in the community whose husbands threatened further violence should they report their abusers. It also supported Gayle Bezaire who abducted her own children when she lost custody to her husband, who had sexually assaulted both her and her daughter.

47. Lynn Smith, interview with the author, Toronto, September 27, 1988, tape recording, LEAF national office.

48. Mary Eberts, "Strategy in Choosing Remedies in Equality cases: A Response to Dale Gibson," in *Righting the Balance*, 348.

49. Unless otherwise indicated, all subsequent references to Mary Eberts are to an interview with the author, Toronto, April 26, 1988.

50. Lynn Smith, interview with the author, Toronto, September 27, 1988.

51. Litigating on behalf of minorities, where racism is directly at issue, presents similar difficulties.

Chapter Three

1. Information on *The Federation of Women Teachers of Ontario v. Margaret Tomen* comes from the files of Mary Eberts, co-counsel on the case. All subsequent references to the case refer to documents contained in her personal files.

2. Beth Symes, round table discussion.

3. Eberts interview April 26, 1988.

4. Summary of The Honourable Mr Justice Ewaschuk, court file no. 2650/86, *FWTAO v. Tomen*, September 16, 1987 (S.C. ONT.).

5. The Charter applies only to state actions.

6. Factum of the Respondent, FWTAO, *FWTAO v. Tomen*, n.d., (S.C. ONT.), 46-47.

7. Affidavit of Monica Towson, January 26, 1987 (S.C. ONT.), *FWTAO v. Tomen.*

8. Cross examination of Mary Hill by Mary Eberts, court file no. 2650/86, February 10, 1987 (S.C. ONT.), *FWTAO v. Tomen.*

9. *Ibid.*, 13.

10. Affidavit of Mary Hill, court file no. 2650/86, n.d. (S.C. ONT.), *FWTAO v. Tomen:* 6.

11. Cross examination of Ross Andrew by Mary Eberts, court file no. 2650/86, February 9, 1987 (S.C. ONT.), *FWTAO v. Tomen.*

12. Factum of the Respondent, FWTAO, 25.

13. Eberts interview April 26, 1988.

14. Affidavit of Catharine MacKinnon, January 27, 1987 (S.C. ONT.), *FWTAO v. Tomen.*

15. Affidavit of Lorenne Clark, January 24, 1987 (S.C. ONT.), *FWTAO v. Tomen.*

16. Affidavit of Margrit Eichler, February 4, 1987 (S.C. ONT.), *FWTAO v. Tomen:* 6.

17. *Ibid.*, 7-14.

18. Affidavit of Ruth Anker Heyer, Oslo, Norway, January 5, 1987; Affidavit of Monique Marti, Geneva, Switzerland, January 24, 1987 (S.C. ONT.), *FWTAO v. Tomen.*

19. Affidavit of Alice Cook, January 16, 1987 (S.C. ONT.), *FWTAO v. Tomen:* 3-4.

20. Affidavit of Janet Pollack, February 3, 1987 (S.C. ONT.), *FWTAO v. Tomen.*

21. Affidavit of Dale Spender, February 2, 1987 (S.C. ONT.), *FWTAO v. Tomen:* 10.

22. Affidavit of Margaret Littlewood, January 13, 1987 (S.C. ONT.), *FWTAO v. Tomen:* 17.

23. Affidavit of Margaret Beattie, January 20, 1987 (S.C. ONT.), *FWTAO v. Tomen.*

24. Affidavit of Jill Conway, February 2, 1987 (S.C. ONT.), *FWTAO v. Tomen:* 3.

25. Affidavit of Joy Parr, January 14, 1987 (S.C. ONT.), *FWTAO v. Tomen.*

26. Affidavit of Marguerite Cassin, January 29, 1987 (S.C. ONT.), *FWTAO v. Tomen:* 11.

27. *Ibid.*

28. *Ibid.*, 37.

29. Affidavit of Sylvia Gold, January 26, 1987 (S.C. ONT.), *FWTAO v. Tomen:* 4.

30. Affidavit of Douglas Allen Penny, January 20, 1987 (S.C. ONT.), *FWTAO v. Tomen.*

31. Affidavit of Florence Henderson, February 3, 1987 (S.C. ONT.), *FWTAO v. Tomen.*

32. Affidavit of Joan Wescott, January 30, 1987 (S.C. ONT.), *FWTAO v. Tomen.*

33. West, "Jurisprudence and Gender," 70.

34. Eberts interview April 26, 1988.

35. The Charter can be invoked to challenge laws, or the regulations that spring from them. The by-laws of the teachers' federations were considered by the judge to fall outside of the definition of laws and regulations passed by the legislature, that is, they were considered regulations privately made.

36. Memorandum of Law of Christine Davies, Vancouver registry no. A870414, n.d. (B.C.S.C.), *Davies v. Century Oils:* 5.

37. Factum of the Appellant, Susan Brooks, Patricia Allen, Patricia Dixon, and the Manitoba Human Rights Commission, n.d. (S.C.C.), *Brooks, Allen, Dixon v. Canada Safeway.*

38. *Davies v. Century Oils,* Vancouver registry no. A870414, Judgement – January 28, 1988, Oppal J. (B.C.S.C.): 2-3.

39. Factum of the Intervenor, the Women's Legal Education and Action Fund, n.d. (S.C.C.), *Brooks, Allen, Dixon v. Canada Safeway:* 3.

40. *Ibid.,* 4.

41. Memorandum of Christine Davies: 11.

42. Factum of the Intervenor, LEAF, *Brooks, Allen, Dixon:* 11.

43. *Ibid.,* 7

44. *Brooks, Allen, Dixon v. Canada Safeway,* court file no. 20131, Judgment – May 4, 1989, Dickson J. (S.C.C.): 5.

45. *Davies v. Century Oils,* Vancouver registry no. A870414, Judgement – January 28, 1988, Oppal J. (B.C.S.C.): 10.

46. Carol Smart, "'There is of course the distinction created by nature'," 101.

47. *Brown v. Klachefsky,* suit no. 400/87, Judgment – January 8, 1988, O'Sullivan, Huband, Philp JJ.A. (MAN. C.A.): 2.

48. *Brown v. Klachefsky,* Decision on a motion for intervention, suit no. 400/87, November 19, 1987, Huband J.A. (MAN. C.A.): 6.

49. *Brown v. Klachefsky,* Judgment, January 8, 1988: 4.

50. *Ibid.,* 2.

51. An Alberta court has recently ruled the opposite way in the case of a mother obliged by remarriage to make her home in another city. The judge in the case ruled that "in the best interest of the children," the children were to stay with their father because they would then be able to stay in the same school, have the same friends, etc. Separation from a mother with whom they had lived was not considered to be as destablilizing as separation from a familiar environment and the fact that more women than men faced the dilemma of moving was not considered pertinent. Dorothy Lipovenko, "Child Stability More Important Than Parental Bond, Court Rules," *The Globe and Mail,* March 17, 1989, A3. See also Queen v. Wald, 23 February 1989, *Alberta Reports* (Court of Appeal): 140.

52. LEAF supported Bezaire by contributing towards the costs of hiring Phyllis Chesler, a well-known American feminist who testified about similar custody disputes in the United States. For an account of the Bezaire case see Susan Crean, *In the Name of the Fathers* (Toronto: Amanita Enterprises, 1988), 31-35. For an account of American trends see Phyllis Chesler, *Mothers on Trial: The Battle for Children and Custody* (New York: McGraw-Hill Book Co., 1986).

53. Shewchuk v. Ricard, *Western Weekly Reports* 6 (1985): 427-435.

54. Shewchuk v. Ricard, *British Columbia Law Review* 66, (1985): 117.

55. *Ibid.,* 124.

56. Lynn Smith, interview with the author, Toronto, September 27, 1988, tape recording, LEAF national office.

57. Shewchuk v. Ricard, *Western Weekly Review* 4, (1986): 289.

58. *Shewchuk v. Ricard,* Judgment – May 9, 1986, Nemetz J. (B.C.C.A.): 290.

59. Eberts interview April 26, 1988.

60. In Canada, intervenors are seldom awarded the same opportunities enjoyed by the parties to a case. The intervenor's participation is usually restricted to making an oral and a written presentation to the court.

61. *Schachter v. Her Majesty the Queen and Canada Employment and Immigration,* court file no. T2345/86 Judgment – June 7, 1988, Strayer J. (F.C.C.T.D.): 1-4.

62. Eberts interview April 26, 1988.

63. *The Toronto Star,* April 20, 1988.

64. Eberts interview April 26, 1988.

65. Mary Eberts, Personal notes on the *Schachter* trial, personal files in her possession.

66. Affidavit of Julie Davis, March 30, 1988, court file no. T2345/86 (F.C.C.T.D.), *Schachter v. Her Majesty the Queen and Canada Employment and Immigration:* 3.

67. Mary Eberts, Personal notes on the *Schachter* trial.

68. Affidavit of Karyn Kaufman and Murray Enkin, court file no. T2345/86 (F.C.C.T.D.), *Schachter v. Her Majesty the Queen and Canada Employment and Immigration:* 4.

69. Affidavit of Dr Marsden G. Wagner, June, 1987, court file no. T2345/86 (F.C.C.T.D.), *Schachter v. Her Majesty the Queen and Canada Employment and Immigration:* 2.

70. Mary Eberts, Trial notes on the *Schachter* trial.

71. Examination for discovery – Joseph Verbruggen, court file no. T2345/86, *Schachter v. Her Majesty the Queen and Canada Employment and Immigration,* (F.C.C.T.D.).

72. Mary Eberts, verbatim notes on Roslyn Levine's arguments.

73. Mary Eberts, Trial notes on the *Schachter* case.

74. *Schachter v. Her Majesty the Queen and Canada Employment and Immigration,* Judgement – June 7, 1988, Strayer J. (F.C.C.T.D.).

75. *Ibid.,* 32.

76. New unemployment insurance legislation came into effect in November 1990 under which parental leave is available to either parent for six months following the birth of a child.

77. Statement of Claim of Lucie Richardson and Leslie Taylor, OSSOMM, September, 1985 (ALTA. C.Q.B., *OSSOMM v. Her Majesty the Queen:* 2.

78. Statement of Defence, Frank Iacobucci, February 12, 1986 (F.C.C.T.D.), *OSSOMM v. Her Majesty the Queen:* 2.

79. *Ibid.,* 4.

80. Harvie André, Oral testimony in Canada, *Proceedings of the Standing Committee on National Defence,* Issue No. 15, June 5, 1986 (Ottawa: Ministry of Supply and Services, 1986): 15.

81. *Ibid.,* 18.

82. *Ibid.,* 26.

83. Gwen Brodsky, Oral testimony in Canada, *Proceedings of the Standing Committee on National Defence*, Issue No. 15, June 12, 1986: 11.

84. Ann Scales, "The Women's Peace Movement and Law: Feminist Jurisprudence as Oxymoron." Lecture delivered in the Legal Theory Workshop Series, University of Toronto, February 26, 1988. This presentation has been revised and published as "Militarism, Male Dominance and Law: Feminist Jurisprudence as Oxymoron," *Harvard Women's Law Journal* 12 (1989): 25-73.

85. *Ibid.*

86. *Ibid.*, 23.

87. *Ibid.*, 25.

88. Cynthia Enloe, *Does Khaki Become You?* (London: Pluto Press, 1983), 6.

89. Leslie V. Taylor, Oral testimony in Canada, *Proceedings of the Standing Committee on National Defence*, Issue No. 16, June 19, 1986: 14.

90. *Ibid.*, 16.

91. Lucie Richardson, Oral testimony in Canada, *Proceedings of the Standing Committee on National Defence*, Issue No. 16, June 19, 1986: 13.

92. Gwen Brodsky, LEAF litigation director, Oral testimony in Canada, *Proceedings of the Standing Committee on National Defence*, Issue No. 15, June 12, 1986.

93. Desmond Morton *et al.*, "The Regulation of Political Activities in Canadian Forces Establishments," a report of an advisory group to the Minister of National Defence, Mississauga, August 14, 1987.

Chapter Four

1. David Cole, referring to the approach taken by Ruth Bader Ginsberg and the American Civil Liberties Union Women's Rights Project. "Strategies of Difference: Litigating for Women's Rights in a Man's World," *Law and Inequality* 2 (1984): 59.

2. Boyle, "Sexual Assault and the Feminist Judge," 100.

3. Andrews's case was taken up by Gorel Elizabeth Kinersly when his status as a non-citizen changed during the course of the case's progress through the legal system.

4. Andrews v. Law Society of British Columbia, *Western Weekly Reports* 4 (1986): 242-261. Intervenors for the appellants were the Attorneys General of Ontario, Quebec, Nova Scotia, Saskatchewan, Alberta, and the Federation of Law Societies of Canada. Intervenors for the respondents Mark David Andrews and Gorel

Elizabeth Kinersly were LEAF, the Coalition of Provincial Organizations of the Handicapped, the Canadian Association of University Teachers, and the Ontario Confederation of University Faculty Associations.

5. *Schachter v. Her Majesty the Queen and Canada Employment and Immigration Commission,* court file no. T2345/86 Judgment – June 7, 1988, Strayer J. (F.C.C.T.D.): 11.

6. Factum of the Intervenor, the Women's Legal Education and Action Fund, *Andrews v. the Law Society of British Columbia* September 22, 1987 (S.C.C.): 32.

7. *Ibid.,* 5.

8. *Ibid.,* 10.

9. *Ibid.,* 25.

10. Mary Eberts, Trial Notes for the *Andrews* case, personal files in her possession.

11. *Ibid.*

12. Factum of the Intervenor, LEAF, *Andrews v. The Law Society of British Columbia:* 23.

13. Round table discussion.

14. Eberts interview April 26, 1988.

15. *The Toronto Star,* February 3, 1989.

16. Dissenting Opinion of The Honourable Mr Justice McIntyre, in *Andrews v. The Law Society of British Columbia,* judgment – February 2, 1989, Wilson J. (S.C.C.): 10.

17. *Ibid.,* 19.

18. *Ibid.,* 30.

19. Editorial, *The Toronto Star,* February 18, 1989.

20. Factum of the Intervenor, the Women's Legal Education and Action Fund, *Janzen/ Govereau v. Platy Enterprises* June, 1988 (S.C.C.): 1.

21. Decision of The Honourable Mr Justice Huband referred to in the Factum of the Intervenor, the Women's Legal Education and Action Fund, *Janzen/ Govereau v. Platy Enterprises:* 11-13.

22. *Ibid.,* 6.

23. *Ibid.,* 8, 9, 16.

24. *Janzen/ Govereau v. Platy Enterprises,* court file no. 20241, Judgment – May 4, 1989, Dickson J. (S.C.C.): 5.

25. In an interview with the author on May 11, 1989, Christie Jefferson described the extensive consultations that have taken place on these two cases, describing four cross-national consultations on cases challenging the rape shield laws.

26. Grange J. A., Judgement in the Supreme Court of Ontario, Court of Appeal, Heard January 12-14, 1987: 4.

27. *Seaboyer/ Gayme v. Her Majesty the Queen*, judgment – November 22, 1985, Galligan J. (TORONTO WEEKLY COURT, S.C. ONT.).

28. *Seaboyer/ Gayme v. Her Majesty the Queen*, Judgment – n.d., Grange, J. (C.A.S.C. ONT.): 34.

29. Christie Jefferson, interview with the author, Toronto, May 11, 1989.

30. Affidavit of LEAF in *Gayme*, quoted in *Leaf Lines* 2, 4 (February 1989): 3.

31. *Ibid.*, 3.

32. Christie Jefferson, interview with the author, Toronto, May 11, 1989.

33. Susan Estrich, *Real Rape* (Cambridge, Mass.: Harvard University Press, 1987), 5-6.

34. *Ibid.*, 24-25.

35. *Ibid.*, 102.

36. Affidavit of Alan Borovoy, General Counsel for the Canadian Civil Liberties Association, December 16, 1986 (S.C. ONT.), *Seaboyer/ Gayme v. Her Majesty the Queen.*

37. Quoted in *The Globe and Mail*, January 7, 1987.

38. Summary provided in *Canadian Newpapers v. Her Majesty the Queen*, court no. 19298, Judgment – September 1, 1988, Lamer J. (S.C.C.): 8-9.

39. Memorandum of Argument Submitted on Behalf of the Respondent, Canadian Newspaper, n.d. (S.C.C.), court no. 19298, *Canadian Newpapers v. Her Majesty the Queen.*

40. Michael Grieve, "Rape Victims in Court. Is Anonymity Their Right?," *Chatelaine* (June 1988): 40-42.

41. The seven groups who signed affidavits requesting intervention along with LEAF were: The Barbara Schlifer Commemorative Clinic providing legal and counselling support to victims of sexual violence; the Metropolitan Toronto Special Committee on Child Abuse; the Metro Action Committee on Public Violence Against Women and Children (METRAC); Women's College Hospital Sexual Assault Care Centre Team (S.A.C.C.); *Broadside*, a feminist newspaper; *Women Healthsharing*, a feminist

magazine; the Ontario Coalition of Rape Crisis Centres. Affidavit of Christie Jefferson, October 20, 1987 (s.c.c.), *Her Majesty the Queen v. Canadian Newspapers.*

42. Factum of the Intervenor, the Women's Legal Education and Action Fund, *Canadian Newpapers Company Ltd. v. Her Majesty the Queen* February 17, 1988 (s.c.c.): 3.

43. *Ibid.*, 5.

44. *Ibid.*, 6.

45. *Ibid.*, 9.

46. *Ibid.*, 11.

47. *Ibid.*, 11.

48. The balcony rapist case was filed under the pseudonym Jane Doe, *Statement of Claim*, No. 21670/87, n.d. (s.c. ONT.), *Jane Doe v. Metropolitan Toronto Police.*

49. *Ibid*, 13.

50. Lynn Smith, interview with the author, Toronto, September 27, 1988.

51. Christie Jefferson, interview with the author, Toronto, May 11, 1989; Oral decision of the Supreme Court of Ontario, *Jane Doe v. Board of Commissioners of Police for the Municipality of Metropolitan Toronto, Jack Marks, Kim Derry and William Cameron,* Henry J., February 22, 1989.

52. Mary O'Brien, *The Politics of Reproduction* (London: Routledge and Kegan Paul Ltd., 1981), 192.

53. *Baby R. v. The Superintendent of Family and Child Services,* Vancouver registry no. A872582, Judgment – August 5, 1988, MacDonell J. (B.C.S.C.).

54. *Baby R. v. The Superintendent of Family and Child Services,* Vancouver registry no. 876215, Judgment – September 3, 1987, Davis J. (B.C.P.C.).

55. This information is based on an interview with Lynn Smith, LEAF counsel advising on the *Baby R.* case and on an article by Suzanne Zwarun, "Fetus's Rights vs. Mother's Rights," *Chatelaine* (January 1988): 53, 92.

56. Lynn Smith, interview with the author, Toronto, September 27, 1988.

57. Affidavit of Katherine P. Young, member of the legal committee of the West Coast LEAF Association, October 29, 1987, Vancouver registry no. A872582 (B.C.S.C.), *Baby R. v. The Superintendent of Family and Child Services.*

58. *Reasons for Judgement,* The Honourable Mr Justice MacDonell: 13.

59. Rosalind Pollack Petchesky, "Foetal Images: The Power of Visual Culture in the Politics of Reproduction," in *Reproductive Technologies. Gender, Motherhood and Medicine,* 63.

60. *Ibid.,* 78.

61. *Morgentaler v. the Queen,* Judgment – January 28, 1988 (s.c.c.), reprinted in eds., Shelagh Day and Stan Persky, *The Supreme Court of Canada Decision on Abortion* (Vancouver: New Star Books, 1988), 24-179.

62. Supplementary Affidavit of Mary Eberts, September 28, 1987 (s.c.c.), *Borowski v. The Attorney General of Canada.*

63. Affidavit of Constance Gwendolyn Landolt, May 5, 1988 (s.c.c.), *Borowski v. The Attorney General of Canada.*

64. Factum of the Appellant, Joseph Borowski, *Borowski v. The Attorney General of Canada,* November 18, 1987 (s.c.c.): 3, 8-9.

65. Mary Eberts, Trial notes for the *Borowski* case, personal files in her possession.

66. *Ibid.*

67. Factum of the Intervenor, the Women's Legal Education and Action Fund, court file no. 20411, *Borowski v. The Attorney General of Canada,* September 14, 1988 (s.c.c.): 1.

68. Petchesky, "Foetal Images," 79.

69. Factum of the Intervenor, the Women's Legal Education and Action Fund: 16.

70. *Borowski v. The Attorney General of Canada,* no. 20411, Judgment – March 9, 1989, Sopinka J. (s.c.c.).

71. In 1986, two midwives, Sullivan and Lemay, were convicted of criminal negligence in causing harm to a foetus whose mother survived. *Criminal Reports* 55 (1986): 48 (b.c.s.c.). The decision was overturned two years later. *British Columbia Law Reports* 31 (1988): 145. The case was appealed to the Supreme Court of Canada and was heard on October 19, 1990. LEAF intervened.

72. Petchesky, "Foetal Images," 63.

73. Bill C-43, *An Act respecting abortion,* 2d sess., 34th Parl., 1989, was defeated in the Senate Jan. 31, 1991. If passed, it would have re-criminalized abortion.

74. Derek Ferguson, "Pro-life Crusader vows Judicial War," *The Toronto Star,* March 10, 1989, A1.

75. Robert Matas, "Tearful Abortion Foes Describe Frustration," *The Globe and Mail*, March 3, 1989, A5.

76. *Morgentaler v. The Queen:* 133.

77. Petchesky, "Foetal Images," 79.

Conclusion

1. Alice Walker, "Silver Writes," *In Search of Our Mothers' Gardens* (San Diego: Harcourt Brace Jovanovich, 1984), 336.

2. A question posed by Lynn Smith in an interview with the author, Toronto, September 27, 1988.

3. *Ibid.*

4. The information on the progress of the spouse-in-the-house cases comes from Helena Orton, currently LEAF's litigation director and also the past member of the Ottawa-based group Women for Justice who first brought the case to LEAF's attention. Interview with the author, Toronto, June 9, 1988.

5. Ian Scott quoted by Cristin Schmitz, "Consider Economic Cost of Charter Remedies: Ont. A.G.," in *Ontario Lawyers Weekly* 8, 30 (December 1988): 24.

6. Helena Orton, interview with the author, Toronto, June 7, 1988, tape recording, LEAF national office.

7. Schneider, "Dialectic," 622-23.

8. Kathleen Lahey, "Civil Remedies for Women: Catching the Critical Edge," *Resources for Feminist Research* 17, 3 (September, 1988): 92.

9. The factum prepared for submission to the Supreme Court of Ontario on behalf of two domestic workers challenging these regulations gives the examples of the two plaintiffs: Melita Chittenden was paid $827.50 a month for seventy hours of work per week, with $238 deducted for room and board. Her hourly wage was therefore $2.73, well below Ontario's minimum wage of $4.25. Similarly, Avelina Villeneuva worked 87 hours for $710 per month, an hourly wage of $1.88. Applicant's Factum, draft in Mary Eberts's possession.

10. Employers quoted by Sarah Jane Growe, "The Difficulties with Domestics," *The Toronto Star*, May 21, 1988, G1.

11. In my interview on May 11, 1989, with Christie Jefferson, LEAF's executive director, she reported that, in her view, considerable progress had been made in this direction.

12. Elizabeth Spelman, *Inessential Woman. Problems of Exclusion in Feminist Thought* (Boston: Beacon Press, 1988), 75.

13. Fran Sugar, "Entrenched Social Catastrophe. Native Women in Prison," *Canadian Woman Studies/ Les Cahiers de la Femme* 10, 2&3 (Summer/Fall 1989): 87-89.

14. Canadian Advisory Council on the Status of Women, *Canadian Charter Equality Rights for Women. One Step Forward or Two Steps Back?*, prepared by Gwen Brodsky and Shelagh Day (Ottawa: Ministry of Supply and Services, 1989).

15. In 1989, the federal government made clear to LEAF its intention to cut its contributions to LEAF by 15%. The Court challenges program, under which LEAF and other disadvantaged groups apply for funding, came to an end in 1989. Christie Jefferson, interview with the author, Toronto, May 11, 1989.

16. Mandel, *The Charter of Rights and The Legalization of Politics in Canada*, 267.

17. Marjorie Cohen had identified the same line of argument I refer to here in reference to the *Schachter* case as operative in the case of John McInnis, a father who wanted to claim the maternity benefits of his wife who died in childbirth. "Giving Fathers an Equal Break," *The Globe and Mail*, February 29, 1988, A7.

18. Mandel, *The Charter of Rights and The Legalization of Politics*, 310.

19. Rick Haliechuk, "Women's Class Discriminatory, Men's Group Complaint Says," *The Toronto Star*, February 16, 1988.

20. Carol Smart, "Marriage, Divorce and Women's Economic Dependency: A Discussion of the Politics of Private Maintenance," in D. A. Freeman, ed., *The State, The Law and The Family* (London: Tavistock, 1984), 10.

21. Alan Hutchinson, "Charter Litigation and Social Change: Legal Battles and Social Wars," in Robert Sharpe, ed., *Charter Litigation* (Toronto: Butterworths, 1987), 378.

22. Editorial, *The Globe and Mail*, March 15, 1988.

23. The men's rights movement includes such groups as The Canadian Council for Family Rights; Fathers for Justice; Fathers and Children: Their Society; The Canadian Council for Co-parenting; The Organization for the Protection of Children's Rights.

24. Reported by Louise Lamb, *Jurisfemme* 18, 1 (June, 1987): 24.

25. Ross Virgin, as interviewed by Peter Cheney, "Waging War on Feminism," *The Toronto Star*, February 16, 1988.

26. Susan Crean, *In the Name of The Fathers. The Story Behind Child Custody*, 135.

27. Scales, "The Women's Peace Movement and Law," 12.

28. *Ibid.*, 12-13.

29. Riley, "Am I That Name?," 16.

30. Adrienne Rich, "Women and Honor: Some Notes on Lying," in *On Lies, Secrets, and Silence. Selected Prose 1966-1978* (New York: W.W. Norton, 1979), 190.

31. *Ibid.*, 192.

SELECTED BIBLIOGRAPHY

Abella, Judge Rosalie Silberman. *Equality in Employment. A Royal Commission Report.* Ottawa: Ministry of Supply and Services, 1984.

————. *Research Studies of the Commission on Equality in Employment.* Ottawa: Ministry of Supply and Services, 1985.

————. "The Dynamic Nature of Equality." In *Equality and Judicial Neutrality,* eds. Sheilah L. Martin and Kathleen Mahoney, 3-10. Toronto: Carswell, 1987.

————. "Equality, the Public, and the Legal System." *Queen's Quarterly* 95, 4 (Winter 1988): 769-779.

Adamson, Nancy, Linda Briskin, and Margaret McPhail. *Feminist Organizing For Change. The Contemporary Women's Movement in Canada.* Toronto: Oxford University Press, 1988.

Aitkins, Susan, and Brenda Hoggett. *Women and the Law.* Oxford: Basil Blackwell, 1984.

Alcoff, Linda. "Cultural Feminism Versus Poststructuralism." *Signs* 13, 3 (Spring 1988): 405-436.

Appelle, Christine. "The New Parliament of Women: A Study of the National Action Committee on the Status of Women." M.A. thesis, Carleton University, Ottawa, 1987.

Ashe, Marie. "Mind's Opportunity: Birthing A Poststructuralist Feminist Jurisprudence." *Syracuse Law Review* 38 (1987): 1129-1173.

————. "Law-Language of Maternity: Discourse Holding Nature in Contempt." *New England Law Review* 22 (March 1988): 521-559.

Atcheson, M. Elizabeth. "Section 15 – Equality Rights General Clause." In *The Study Day Papers*. Toronto: Charter of Rights Education Fund, January 15, 1983.

Axworthy, Thomas S. "Liberalism and Equality." In *Equality and Judicial Neutrality,* eds. Sheilah L. Martin and Kathleen Mahoney, 43-49. Toronto: Carswell, 1987.

Baines, Beverly. "Women, Human Rights and the Constitution." Paper prepared for the Canadian Advisory Council on the Status of Women. Ottawa: August 1980, revised October, 1980. In *Women and the Constitution In Canada*, eds. Audrey Doerr and Micheline Carrier, 31-63. Ottawa: Ministry of Supply and Services, 1981.

———. "Women and the Law." In *Changing Patterns. Women in Canada*, eds. Sandra Burt, Lorraine Code, and Lindsay Dorney, 157-183. Toronto: McClelland and Stewart, 1988.

Baker, Gale S. "Is Equality Enough?" *Hypatia* 2, 1 (Winter 1987): 63-70.

Barrett, Michèle. "The Concept of 'Difference'." *Feminist Review* 26 (July 1987): 27-41.

Bartholomew, Amy, and Susan Boyd. "Toward A Political Economy of Law." In *The New Canadian Political Economy*, eds. Wallace Clement and Glen Williams, 212-239. Montreal: McGill University Press, 1989.

Bartky, Sandra Lee. "Foucault, Femininity, and the Modernization of Patriarchal Power." In *Feminism and Foucault. Reflections on Resistance*, eds. Irene Diamond and Lee Quinby, 61-86. Boston: Northeastern University Press, 1988.

Bashevkin, Sylvia B. *Toeing the Lines. Women and Party Politics in English Canada*. Toronto: University of Toronto Press, 1985.

———. "Independence versus Partisanship: Dilemmas in the Political History of Women in English Canada." In *Rethinking Canada*, eds. Veronica Strong-Boag and Anita Clair Fellman, 246-275. Toronto: Copp Clark Pitman Ltd., 1986.

Bayevsky, Anne. "Defining Equality Rights." In *Equality Rights and the Canadian Charter of Rights and Freedoms*, eds. Anne Bayevsky and Mary Eberts, 1-78. Toronto: Carswell, 1985.

———. "Defining Equality Rights Under the Charter." In *Equality and Judicial Neutrality*, eds. Sheilah L. Martin and Kathleen Mahoney, 106-114. Toronto: Carswell, 1987.

Berger, Margaret. *Litigation on Behalf of Women. A review for the Ford Foundation*. New York: Ford Foundation, May, 1980.

Bird, Florence. *Report of the Royal Commission on the Status of Women*. Ottawa: Ministry of Supply and Services, 1970.

Black, Naomi. "The Canadian Women's Movement: The Second Wave." In *Changing Patterns. Women in Canada*, eds. Sandra Burt, Lorraine Code, and Lindsay Dorney, 80-102. Toronto: McClelland and Stewart, 1988.

Black, William. "From Intent to Effect: New Standards in Human Rights." *Canadian Human Rights Reporter* (February 1980): c1-c5.

———. *Employment Equality: A Systemic Approach*. Ottawa: Human Rights Research and Education Centre, University of Ottawa, 1986.

Bouchier, David. *The Feminist Challenge. The Movement for Women's Liberation in Britain and the U.S.* London: Macmillan, 1983.

Boyd, Susan, and Elizabeth A. Sheehy. "Feminist Perspectives on Law: Canadian Theory and Practice." *Canadian Journal of Women and the Law* 2 (1986): 1-51.

Boyer, Patrick J. *Equality For All. Report of The Parliamentary Committee on Equality Rights*. Ottawa: Queen's Printer, 1985.

Boyle, Christine. "Sexual Assault and the Feminist Judge." *Canadian Journal of Women and the Law* 1 (1985): 93-107.

———. *Sexual Assault*. Toronto: Carswell, 1985.

———. "A Feminist Approach to Criminal Defences." Unpublished draft in the author's possession, July 1988.

Boyle, Christine, and Shiela Noonan. "Prostitution and Pornography: Beyond Formal Equality." In *Charterwatch*, eds. Christine Boyle *et al.*, 225-265. Toronto: Carswell, 1986.

Brodsky, Gwen. "Women and The Canadian Charter of Rights and Freedoms." In *The Canadian Woman's Legal Guide*, ed. M.J. Dymond, 319-336. Toronto: Doubleday, 1987.

Burt, Sandra D. "Women and the Canadian Charter of Rights and Freedoms: A Case Study of Women's Groups and Canadian Public Policy." Paper prepared for presentation at the 55th annual meeting of the Canadian Political Science Association, University of British Columbia, June 7, 1983. Photocopy.

———. "Women's Issues and the Women's Movement in Canada Since 1970." In *The Politics of Gender, Ethnicity and Language in Canada*, eds. Alan Cairns and Cynthia Williams, 111-169. Toronto: University of Toronto Press, 1985.

Cain, Maureen. "Realism, Feminism, Methodology, and Law." *International Journal of the Sociology of Law* 14 (1986): 255-267.

Canada. Department of Justice. *Toward Equality. The Response to the Report of the Parliamentary Committee on Equality Rights.* Ottawa: Ministry of Supply and Services, 1986.

Canadian Advisory Council on the Status of Women (CACSW). "Summary of the Proceedings of the Conference on the Constitution. Women and the Constitution: The Next Five Years." Ottawa: CACSW, May 29, 30, 1981.

————. *Women and Legal Action.* Report prepared by M. Elizabeth Atcheson, Mary Eberts, and Beth Symes, with Jennifer Stoddart. Ottawa: CACSW, October 1984.

————. *Canadian Charter Equality Rights for Women. One Step Forward or Two Steps Back?* by Gwen Brodsky and Shelagh Day. Ottawa: Ministry of Supply and Services, 1989.

Canadian Bar Association. "A Blueprint for Implementation of Constitutional Equality Rights." Submission to the Parliamentary Special Committee on Equality Rights, Ottawa, June 17, 1985.

Canadian Broadcasting Corporation. "New Directions In Criminal Law." Transcript of the radio program "Ideas," September 28, October 5, 12, 1987. Quebec: CBC Transcripts, P.O. Box 6440, Station A, Montreal.

————. "The People's Charter." Transcript of the radio program "Ideas," April 11, 18, 1988. Quebec: CBC Transcripts, P.O. Box 6440, Station A, Montreal.

Cetnar, Maria, and Jane Haddad. "Recent Changes in Welfare Policy in Selected Canadian Provinces." Occasional Paper No. 9, Centre for Women's Studies in Education, The Ontario Institute for Studies in Education, Toronto, 1985.

Charter of Rights Coalition (Vancouver). "What was said: The Submissions of Women's Groups to the Parliamentary Committee on Equality Rights." Eds. Janet Kee and Nadine McDonnell. Vancouver: Charter of Rights Coalition, 1986.

Charter of Rights Educational Fund. *Report on the Statute Audit Project.* Toronto: Charter of Rights Education Fund, 1985.

Chesler, Phyllis. *Mothers On Trial. The Battle for Children and Custody.* New York: McGraw-Hill Book Co., 1986.

————. *Sacred Bond. The Legacy of Baby M.* New York: Times Books, 1988.

Cole, David. "Getting There: Reflections on Trashing From Feminist Jurisprudence And Critical Theory." *Harvard Women's Law Journal* 8 (1985) : 59-91.

————. "Strategies of Difference: Litigating for Women's Rights in a Man's World." *Law and Inequality* 2 (1984) : 33-95.

Cole, Susan G. *Pornography And The Sex Crisis.* Toronto: Amanita Enterprises, 1989.

———. "Meech Lake: Troubled Waters." *Broadside* 9, 2 (November 1987): 3.

Collins, Anne. *The Big Evasion: Abortion, the Issue That Won't Go Away.* Toronto: Lester and Orpen Dennys Ltd., 1985.

Collins, Larry D. "The Politics of Abortion: Trends in Canadian Fertility Policy." *Atlantis* 7, 2 (Spring/Printemps 1982): 2-20.

Costain, Anne N. "Representing Women: The Transition from Social Movement to Interest Group." In *Women, Power and Policy,* ed. Ellen Boneparth, 19-31. New York: Pergamon Press, 1982.

Cover, Robert. "Nomos and Narrative." *Harvard Law Review* 97, 1 (November 1983): 4-68.

Dalton, Clare. "An Essay in the Deconstruction of Contract Doctrine." *The Yale Law Journal* 94, 5 (April 1985): 997-1114.

Dawson, T. Brettel, "Sexual Assault and Past Sexual Conduct of the Primary Witness: The Construction of Relevance." Unpublished paper in the author's possession, 1988.

———. "Against Her Will." *Broadside* 10, 1 (January 1989): 3.

———. "Submitting to the Judge." *Broadside* 10, 2 (February 1989): 3

———. "Fetal Rights, Maternal Wrongs." *Broadside* 10, 3 (December 1988): 3.

Day, Shelagh. "Government Charter Audits: Will They Address The Equality Problems of Women?" In *The Study Day Papers,* Toronto, Charter of Rights Education Fund, February 19, 1983.

Day, Shelagh, and Stan Persky, eds. *The Supreme Court of Canada Decision on Abortion.* Vancouver: New Star Books, 1988.

de Jong, Katherine J. "Sexual Equality: Interpreting Section 28." In *Equality Rights and the Canadian Charter of Rights and Freedoms,* eds. Anne Bayevsky and Mary Eberts, 493-528. Toronto: Carswell, 1985.

———. "Charter of Rights and Freedoms." In *The Study Day Papers.* Toronto: Charter of Rights Education Fund, January 15, 1983.

De Lauretis, Teresa. *Technologies of Gender. Essays on Theory, Film and Fiction.* Bloomington and Indianapolis: Indiana University Press, 1987.

Eberts, Mary. "Women and Constitutional Renewal." Paper prepared for the Canadian Advisory Council on the Status of Women. Ottawa: September, 1980. In *Women and the Constitution,* eds. Audrey Doerr and Micheline Carrier, 3-27. Ottawa: Ministry of Supply and Services, 1981.

————. "Preliminary Study. Equality Rights Under the Canadian Charter of Rights and Freedoms and the Statutes of Canada." Paper prepared for, and with the financial assistance of, Status of Women Canada, Government of Canada, March, 1983.

————. "Sex-Based Discrimination and the Charter." In *Equality Rights and the Canadian Charter of Rights and Freedoms,* eds. Anne Bayevsky and Mary Eberts, 183-229. Toronto: Carswell, 1985.

————. "Making Use of the Charter of Rights." In *Women, The Law and the Economy,* eds. Diane E. Pask *et al.,* 322-348. Toronto: Butterworths, 1985.

————. "The Use of Litigation Under the Canadian Charter of Rights and Freedoms as a Strategy for Achieving Change." In *Minorities and the Canadian State,* eds. Neil Nevitte and Allan Kornberg, 1-53. Oakville, Ontario: Mosaic Press, 1985.

————. "Strategy in Choosing Remedies in Equality Cases: A Response to Dale Gibson." In *Righting the Balance,* eds. Lynn Smith *et al.,* 343-349. Toronto: Carswell, 1986.

————. "A Strategy for Equality Litigation under the Canadian Charter of Rights and Freedoms." In *Litigating the Values of a Nation: The Canadian Charter of Rights and Freedoms,* eds. Joseph M. Weiler and Robin M. Elliot, 411-425. Toronto: Carswell, 1986.

————. "LEAF and the Charter." A Talk at the LEAF luncheon seminar sponsored by Warner-Lambert Canada Inc. and the Metropolitan Toronto Community Foundation, February 26, 1987, Westin Hotel, Toronto. Photocopy.

————. "Risks of Equality Litigation." In *Equality and Judicial Neutrality,* eds. Sheilah L. Martin and Kathleen Mahoney, 89-105. Toronto: Carswell, 1987.

Eisenstein, Zillah. *The Female Body And The Law.* Berkeley: University of California Press, 1988.

Enloe, Cynthia. *Does Khaki Become You?* London: Pluto Press, 1983.

Estrich, Susan. *Real Rape.* Cambridge: Cambridge University Press, 1987.

"Feminist Discourse, Moral Values and the Law – A Conversation." The 1984 James McCormick Mitchell Lecture. *Buffalo Law Review* 34 (1985): 11-87.

Ferguson, Kathy E. *The Feminist Case Against Bureaucracy.* Philadelphia: Temple University Press, 1984.

Ferree, Myra Marx, and Beth B. Hess. *Controversy and Coalition.* Boston: Twayne Publishers, 1985.

Findley, Sue. "Facing the State: The Politics of the Women's Movement Reconsidered." In *Feminism and Political Economy,* eds. Meg Luxton and Heather Jon Maroney, 31-50. Toronto: Methuen, 1987.

Fineman, Martha L. "Implementing Equality: Ideology, Contradiction and Social Change." *Wisconsin Law Review* 4 (1983): 789-886.

Finn, Geraldine. "Beyond Either/Or: Postmodernism And The Politics of My Kind of Feminism." Presented at the workshop on Feminism, Critical Theory and The Canadian Legal System, June 4-7, 1988, Windsor University Faculty of Law, June 1988. Draft.

Flax, Jane. "Postmodernism And Gender Relations in Feminist Theory." *Signs* 12, 4 (Summer 1987): 621-643.

———. "Re-Membering The Selves: Is The Repressed Gendered?" *Michigan Quarterly Review* 26, 1 (Winter 1987): 92-110.

———. "Comment and Reply." *Signs* 14,1 (Autumn 1988): 202-203.

Fogarty, Kenneth H., The Hon. *Equality Rights and Their Limitations in the Charter.* Toronto: Carswell, 1987.

Foucault, Michel. *Power/Knowledge. Selected Interviews and Other Writings. 1972-1977.* Ed. Colin Gordon. Translated by Colin Gordon, Leo Marshall, John Mepham, and Kate Soper. New York: Pantheon Books, 1980.

Fraser, David. "What's Love Got To Do With It? Critical Legal Studies, Feminist Discourse, And The Ethic Of Solidarity." *Harvard Women's Law Journal* 11 (1988): 53-82.

Freeman, Jo. *The Politics of Women's Liberation.* New York: Longman Inc., 1975.

———. "Women and Public Policy: An Overview." In *Women Power and Public Policy,* ed. Ellen Boneparth, 47-67. New York: Pergamon Press, 1982.

Freeman, Michael D. A. "Legal Ideologies, Patriarchal Precedents, and Domestic Violence." In *The State, The Law, and The Family,* ed. Michael D.A. Freeman, 51-78. London: Tavistock, 1984.

Gallagher, Janet. "Prenatal Invasions and Interventions: What's Wrong With Fetal Rights." *Harvard Women's Law Journal* 10 (1987): 9-58.

Gavigan, Shelley A. M. "Women, Law and Patriarchal Relations." In *The Social Dimensions of Law,* ed. Neil Boyd, 101-124. Scarborough: Prentice Hall, 1986.

———. "Women and Abortion in Canada: What's Law Got To Do With It?" In *Feminism and Political Economy. Women's Work, Women's Struggles,* eds. Meg Luxton and Heather Jon Maroney, 263-284. Toronto: Methuen, 1987.

Gibson, Dale. "Accentuating the Positive and Eliminating the Negative: Remedies for Inequality Under the Canadian Charter." In *Righting the Balance*, eds. Lynn Smith *et al.*, 311-341. Toronto: Carswell, 1986.

———. "Canadian Equality Jurisprudence: Year One." In *Equality and Judicial Neutrality*, eds. Sheilah L. Martin and Kathleen Mahoney, 128-150. Toronto: Carswell, 1987.

Gold, Marc Emmett. "Equality Before The Law In The Supreme Court Of Canada: A Case Study." *Osgoode Hall Law Journal* 18, 3 (1980): 337-427.

Gordon, Robert W. "New Developments in Legal Theory." In *The Politics of Law. A Progressive Critique*, ed. David Kairys, 281-293. New York: Pantheon Books, 1982.

Graycar, Regina. "Yes, Virginia There Is Feminist Legal Literature. A Survey of Some Recent Publications." *Australian Journal of Law and Society* 3, (1986): 105-135.

Greer, Edward. "Antonio Gramsci And Legal Hegemony." In *The Politics of Law. A Progressive Critique*, ed. David Kairys, 304-309. New York: Pantheon Books, 1982.

Greschner, Donna. "Judicial Approaches to Equality and Critical Legal Studies." In *Equality and Judicial Neutrality*, eds. Sheilah L. Martin and Kathleen Mahoney, 59-70. Toronto: Carswell, 1987.

Griffin, Susan. *Made From This Earth. Selections From Her Writing*. London: The Women's Press Ltd., 1982.

Guillaumin, Colette. "The Question of Difference." *Feminist Issues* 2, 1 (Spring 1982): 33-52.

Haddad, Jane. "Sexism and Social Policy: The Case of Family Benefits in Ontario." Occasional Paper No. 8, Centre for Women's Studies in Education, The Ontario Institute for Studies In Education, Toronto, 1985.

Handler, Joel F. *Social Movements and The Legal System*. New York: Academic Press, 1978.

Hogg, Peter. "Legislative History in Constitutional Cases." In *Charter Litigation*, ed. Robert Sharpe, 131-158. Toronto: Butterworths, 1987.

Hosek, Chaviva, "Women and the Constitutional Process." In *And No One Cheered*, eds. Keith Banting and Richard Simeon, 280-305. Toronto: Methuen, 1983.

Hughes, Patricia. "Feminist Equality and the Charter: Conflict with Reality?" *Windsor Yearbook of Access to Justice* 5 (1985): 39-101.

Hutchinson, Allan C. "Charter Litigation and Social Change: Legal Battles and Social Wars." In *Charter Litigation*, ed. Robert Sharpe, 357-381. Toronto: Butterworths, 1987.

———. "From Cultural Construction to Historical Deconstruction." A book review of *When Words Lose Their Meaning: Constitutions and Re-Constituions of Language, Character and Community,* by James Boyd White. *The Yale Law Journal* 94 (1984): 209-237.

Jaggar, Alison. *Feminist Politics and Human Nature.* New Jersey: Rowman and Allanheld, 1983.

Jardine, Alice. "Introduction to Julia Kristeva's 'Women's Time'." *Signs* 7, 1 (Autumn 1981): 5-12.

———. *Gynesis. Configurations of Woman and Modernity.* Ithaca: Cornell University Press, 1985.

Kairys, David, ed. *The Politics of Law. A Progressive Critique.* New York: Pantheon Books, 1982.

———. "Legal Reasoning." In *The Politics of Law. A Progressive Critique,* ed. David Kairys, 11-17. New York: Pantheon Books, 1982.

Karst, Kenneth L. "Woman's Constitution." *Duke Law Journal* 3 (June 1984): 447-508.

Kennedy, Duncan. "Legal Education As Training for Hierarchy." In *The Politics of Law. A Progressive Critique,* ed. David Kairys, 40-61. New York: Pantheon Books, 1982.

Klare, Karl. "Law-making as Praxis." *Telos* 40 (1979): 123-135.

Kline, Marlee. "Race, Racism, And Feminist Legal Theory." *Harvard Women's Law Journal* 12 (1989): 115-150.

Kluger, Richard. *Simple Justice. The History of Brown v. Board of Education.* New York: Vintage Books, 1977.

Knox, Rena. "The Politics of Catharine MacKinnon." Unpublished paper in the author's possession, April 17, 1988.

Kome, Penney. *The Taking of Twenty Eight. Women Challenge the Constitution.* Toronto: The Women's Press, 1983.

Kostash, Myrna. "Whose Body? Whose Self? Beyond Pornography." In *Still Ain't Satisfied! Canadian Feminism Today,* eds. Maureen Fitzgerald, Connie Guberman, and Margie Wolfe, 43-54. Toronto: The Women's Press, 1982.

———. *Long Way From Home.* Toronto: James Lorimer and Company, 1980.

Krieger, Linda J. "Through A Glass Darkly: Paradigms of Equality and the Search for A Woman's Jurisprudence." *Hypatia* 2, 1 (Winter 1987): 45-61.

Kristeva, Julia. "Women's Time," Translated by Alice Jardine and Harry Blake. *Signs* 7, 11 (Autumn 1981):13-35.

————. "The System and The Speaking Subject." In *The Kristeva Reader*, ed. Toril Moi, 25-33. Oxford: Basil Blackwell, 1986.

Lafave, Bonnie. "Who's in Control? Eggs, Embryos and Fetal Tissue." *Healthsharing* (Fall 1988): 29-32.

Lahey, Kathleen A. "The Canadian Charter of Rights and Pornography: Toward a Theory of Actual Gender Equality." *New England Law Review* 20, 4 (1984-85): 649-685.

————. "…Until Women Themselves Have Told All That They Have To Tell…" *Osgoode Hall Law Journal* 23, 3 (1985): 519-541.

————. "Feminist Theories of (In)Equality." In *Equality and Judicial Neutrality*, eds. Sheilah L. Martin and Kathleen Mahoney, 71-85. Toronto: Carswell, 1987.

————. "Civil remedies for Women: Catching the Critical Edge." *Resources for Feminist Research/ Documentation sur la Recherche Feministe* 17, 3 (September 1988): 92-95.

Lamb, Louise. "Convicted 'Childnapper' Heads New Fathers' Rights Group." *Jurisfemme* 18, 1 (June 1987): 24.

Lessard, Hester. "The Idea of the 'Private': A Discussion of State Action Doctrine and Separate Sphere Ideology." In *Charterwatch*, ed. Christine Boyle, 107-137. Toronto: Carswell, 1986.

Litchman, Judith L. "The Law of Sex Discrimination in the United States." In *The Study Day Papers*. Toronto: Charter of Rights Education Fund, February 19, 1983.

Littleton, Christine A. "In Search of a Feminist Jurisprudence." *Harvard Women's Law Journal* 10 (1987): 1-7.

Lukes, Steven. *Power: A Radical View*. London: Macmillan, 1974.

Lyotard, Jean-François. *The Post-Modern Condition: A Report on Knowledge*. Translated by Geoff Bennington and Brian Massumi. Minneapolis: University of Minnesota Press, 1986.

MacKinnon, Catharine A. "Making Sex Equality Real." In *Righting the Balance*, eds. Lynn Smith *et al.*, 37-43. Toronto: Carswell, 1986.

————. *Sexual Harassment of Working Women*. New Haven: Yale University Press, 1979.

————. "Feminism, Marxism, Method, and the State: An Agenda for Theory." *Signs* 7, 3 (Spring 1982): 515-544.

————. "Feminism, Marxism, Method, and the State: Toward Feminist Jurisprudence." *Signs* 8, 4 (Summer, 1983): 635-658.

————. *Feminism Unmodified. Discourses on Life and Law.* Cambridge: Harvard University Press, 1987.

Mandel, Michael. *The Charter of Rights and the Legalization of Politics in Canada.* Toronto: Wall and Thompson, Inc., 1989.

Martin, Biddy. "Feminism, Criticism, and Foucault." *New German Critique* 27 (Fall 1982): 3-30.

Martin, Sheilah L. "The Reluctance of the Judiciary to Balance Competing Interests: R. v. Morgentaler in the Ontario Court of Appeal." *Canadian Journal of Women and the Law* 1 (1986): 537.

————. "Morgentaler v. The Queen in the Supreme Court of Canada." *Canadian Journal of Women and the Law* 2 (1987-88): 422-431.

Matsuda, Mari J. "Liberal Jurisprudence and Abstracted Visions of Human Nature: A Feminist Critique of Rawls' Theory of Justice." *New Mexico Law Review* 16 (Fall 1987): 613-630.

May, Larry. *The Morality of Groups.* Indiana: University of Notre Dame Press, 1987.

McDonnell, Kathleen. "Claim No Easy Victories. The Fight for Reproductive Rights." In *Still Ain't Satisfied! Canadian Feminism Today,* eds. Maureen Fitzgerald, Connie Guberman, and Margie Wolfe, 32-43. Toronto: The Women's Press, 1982.

McPhedran, Marilou. "Section 28 – Was it Worth the Fight?" In *The Study Day Papers.* Toronto: Charter of Rights Education Fund, January 15, 1983.

McWilliams, Nancy. "Contemporary Feminism, Consciousness-Raising, and Changing Views of the Political." In *Women In Politics,* ed. Jane S. Jaquette, 157-170. New York: John Wiley & Sons, 1974.

Menkel-Meadow, Carrie. "Portia in a Different Voice: Speculations on a Women's Lawyering Process." *Berkeley Women's Law Journal* 1 (1985): 39-63.

Metro Action Committee On Public Violence Against Women and Children. *Report on Civil Remedies for the Harms of Pornography: An Analysis of Legal Remedies.* Unpublished draft, Toronto, 1989.

Miles, Angela. "Feminist Radicalism in the 1980s (1)." In *Feminism Now: Theory and Practice,* eds. Marilouise Kroker *et al.,* 16-39. Montreal: New World Perspectives, 1985.

Minh-ha, Trinh T. *Woman, Native, Other.* Bloomington and Indianapolis: Indiana University Press, 1989.

Mitchell, Juliet. "Reflections on Twenty Years of Feminism." In *What is Feminism?* eds. Juliet Mitchell and Ann Oakley, 34-48. Oxford: Basil Blackwell, 1986.

Mitchell, Juliet, and Ann Oakley, eds. *What is Feminism?* Oxford: Basil Blackwell, 1986.

Moi, Toril, ed. *The Kristeva Reader.* Oxford: Basil Blackwell, 1986.

Monahan, Patrick J. "A Critics' Guide To The Charter." In *Charter Litigation*, ed. Robert Sharpe, 383-408. Toronto: Butterworths, 1987.

Morgan, Brian G. "Proof of Facts in Charter Litigation." In *Charter Litigation*, ed. Robert Sharpe, 159-186. Toronto: Butterworths, 1987.

Morris, Cerise. "Determination and Thoroughness: The Movement for a Royal Commission on the Status of Women in Canada." *Atlantis* 5, 2 (Spring 1980): 1-21.

Morton, Desmond, Yolande Leblanc, and Michelle Deschenes. "The Regulation of Political Activities in Canadian Forces Establishments." A Report of an Advisory Group to the Minister of National Defence, Mississauga, August 14, 1987.

Mossman, Mary Jane. "Feminism and Legal Method: The Difference It Makes." *Australian Journal of Law and Society* 3 (1986): 30-52.

———. "Gender, Equality, and the Charter." In *Research Studies of the Commission on Equality in Employment*, 299-304. Ottawa: Ministry of Supply and Services, 1985.

Mullarkey, Maureen. "Hard Cop, Soft Cop." A book review of *Intercourse* by Andrea Dworkin, and *Feminism Unmodified*, by Catherine MacKinnon. *The Nation*, (May 30, 1987): 720-726.

National Action Committee on the Status of Women. "Memorandum of Law: Background to the Parliamentary Committee on Equality Rights. Section 15. The Charter of Rights and its Implications for Canadian Women." n.d.

——— "Equality in Employment Under the Charter of Rights and Freedoms: Response of the National Action Committee on the Status of Women to Equality Issues in Federal Law." Prepared and presented by Michelle Swenarchuk, Toronto, June 1985.

———. "Section 15 of the Charter and NAC's Program for Equality." A Brief presented to the Subcommittee on Equality Rights in Toronto, June 18, 1985.

National Association of Women and the Law. "The Charter of Rights and Freedoms. Not Just Words on Paper." A Brief submitted to the Parliamentary Subcommittee on Equality Rights, June 1985.

National Association of Women and the Law. *Jurisfemme* 7, 3 (February 1987); 8, 1 (June 1987); 8, 2 (Fall 1987).

Nye, Andrea. "Woman Clothed With The Sun: Julia Kristeva And The Escape From/To Language." *Signs* 12, 4 (Summer 1987): 664-686.

O'Brien, Mary, and Shiela McIntyre. "Patriarchal Hegemony and Legal Education." *Canadian Journal of Women and the Law* 2 (1986): 69-95.

O'Connor, Karen. *Women's Organizations' Use of the Courts.* Massachusetts: Lexington Books, 1980.

Olsen, Frances E. "The Family And The Market: A Study Of Ideology And Legal Reform." *Harvard Law Review* 7, 96 (May 1983): 1497-1578.

————."The Politics of Family Law." *Law and Inequality* 2 (1984): 1-19.

Ontario Ministry of the Attorney General. *Sources for the Interpretation of Equality Rights Under the Charter.* Government of Ontario, June 1985.

Overall, Christine. "Reproductive Ethics: Feminist and Non-Feminist Approaches." *Canadian Journal of Women and the Law* 1 (1986): 271-278.

Pask, Diane E., Kathleen E. Mahoney, and Catherine A. Brown, eds. *Women, The Law And The Economy.* Toronto: Butterworths, 1985.

Penelope, Julia. "Language and the Transformation of Consciousness." *Law and Inequality* 4 (1986): 379-393.

Petchesky, Rosalind Pollack. "Foetal Images: The Power of Visual Culture in the Politics of Reproduction." In *Reproductive Technologies. Gender, Motherhood and Medicine,* ed. Michelle Stanworth, 57-80. Minneapolis: University of Minnesota Press, 1987.

Petter, Andrew. "The Politics of the Charter." *Supreme Court Law Review* 8 (1986): 473-505.

Polan, Diane. "Toward A Theory of Law and Patriarchy." In *The Politics of Law. A Progressive Critique,* ed. David Kairys, 294-303. New York: Pantheon Books, 1982.

Prentice, Alison *et al. Canadian Women: A History.* Toronto: Harcourt Brace Jovanovich, 1988.

Rawls, John. *A Theory of Justice.* Cambridge, Massachusetts: Harvard University Press, 1971.

Ray, Douglas. *Equalities.* Massachusetts: Harvard University Press, 1981.

Richardson, Joan T. "The Structure of Organizational Instability: The Women's Movement in Montreal 1974-1977." PH.D. diss., New School for Social Research, New York, 1981.

Rifkin, Janet. "Toward A Theory of Law And Patriarchy." *Harvard Women's Law Journal* 3 (1980): 83-95.

Riley, Denise. *"Am I That Name?": Feminism And The Category of 'Women' In History.* Minneapolis: University of Minnesota Press, 1988.

Rodgers, Sanda. "Fetal Rights and Maternal Rights: Is There a Conflict?" *Canadian Journal of Women and the Law* 1 (1986): 456-469.

Rogers, Peter. "Equality, Efficiency and Judicial Restraint: Toward a Dynamic Constitution." In *Charterwatch*, ed. Christine Boyle *et al.*, 139-193. Toronto: Carswell, 1986.

Sandel, Michael J. *Liberalism and the Limits of Justice.* Cambridge: Cambridge University Press, 1982.

Scales, Ann C. "Toward a Feminist Jurisprudence." *Indiana Law Journal* 56, 3 (1980-81): 375-444.

———. "The Women's Peace Movement And Law: Feminist Jurisprudence As Oxymoron." Text of a lecture delivered in the Legal Theory Workshop Series, University of Toronto, February 26, 1988.

———. "Militarism, Male Dominance and Law: Feminist Jurisprudence as Oxymoron?" *Harvard Women's Law Journal* 12 (1989): 25-73.

Scheman, Naomi. "Individualism And The Objects of Psychology." In *Discovering Reality*, eds. Sandra Harding and Merrill B. Hintikka, 225-244. Holland: D. Reidel Publishing Co., 1983.

Schneider, Elizabeth M. "The Dialectic of Rights and Politics: Perspectives From the Women's Movement." *New York University Law Review* 61 (October 1986): 589-652.

———, moderator. "Lesbians, Gays and Feminists at the Bar: Translating Personal Experience into Effective Legal Argument – A Symposium." *Women's Rights Law Reporter* 10, 2-3 (Winter 1988): 107-141.

Scott, Joan W. "Gender: A Useful Category of Historical Analysis." *American Historical Review* 91, 5 (December 1986): 1053-75.

———. *Gender and The Politics of History.* New York: Columbia University Press, 1988.

Sheehy, Elizabeth. "Personal Autonomy and The Criminal Law: Emerging Issues for Women." Background paper prepared for the Canadian Advisory Council on the Status of Women, Ottawa, September, 1987.

Sheppard, Colleen N. "Equality, Ideology and Oppression: Women and the Canadian Charter of Rights and Freedoms." In *Charterwatch*, eds. Christine Boyle *et al.*, 195-223. Toronto: Carswell, 1986.

Sherry, Suzanna. "The Gender of Judges." *Law and Inequality* 4 (1986): 159-169.

Shrofel, Salina M. "Equality Rights and Law Reform in Saskatchewan: An Assessment of the Charter Compliance Process." *Canadian Journal of Women and the Law* 1 (1985): 108.

Simon, Anne E. Review of *The Politics of Law: A Progressive Critique,* ed. by David Kairys. *Women's Rights Law Reporter* 8, 3 (Summer 1985): 199-204.

Singer, Joseph William. "The Player and the Cards: Nihilism and Legal Theory." *The Yale Law Journal* 94, 1 (November 1984): 1-70.

Smart, Carol, and Julia Brophy. "Locating Law: A Discussion of the Place of Law in Feminist Politics." In *Women In Law. Explorations in Law, Family and Sexuality,* eds. Carol Smart and Julia Brophy, 1-20. London: Routledge and Kegan Paul, 1985.

Smart, Carol. "Marriage, Divorce, and Women's Economic Dependency: A Discussion of the Politics of Private Maintainance." In *The State, The Law and The Family,* ed. Michael D.A. Freeman, 9-24. London: Tavistock Publications, 1984.

———. "Feminism and Law: Some Problems of Analysis and Strategy." *International Journal of the Sociology of Law* 14, (1986): 109-123.

———. "Law's Truth/Women's Experience." Unpublished draft, 1987.

———. "'There is of Course the Distinction Dictated by Nature': Law and the Problem of Paternity." In *Reproductive Technologies. Gender, Motherhood And Medicine,* ed. Michelle Stanworth, 98-117. Minneapolis: University of Minnesota Press, 1987.

———. *Feminism and The Power of Law.* London: Routledge, 1989.

Smith, Lynn. "The Effect of the Charter on Sex Discrimination." In *The Study Day Papers.* Toronto: Charter of Rights Education Fund, February 19, 1983.

———. "A New Paradigm for Equality Rights." In *Righting the Balance,* eds. Lynn Smith *et al.,* 353-366. Toronto: Carswell, 1986.

Spender, Dale. *Men's Studies Modified: The Impact of Feminism on the Academic Press.* Oxford: Pergamon Press, 1981.

Stubbs, Margot. "Feminism and Legal Positivism." *Australian Journal of Law and Society* 3 (1986): 63-91.

Swinton, Katherine. "Introduction to the Charter." In *The Study Day Papers.* Toronto: Charter of Rights Education Fund, January 15, 1983.

———. "What do the Courts Want from the Social Sciences?" In *Charter Litigation,* ed. Robert Sharpe, 187-211. Toronto: Butterworths, 1987.

Symes, Beth. "Section 24 – Enforcement Clause." In *The Study Day Papers.* Toronto: Charter of Rights Education Fund, January 15, 1983.

———. "Equality Theories and Maternity Benefits." In *Equality and Judicial Neutrality,* eds. Sheilah L. Martin and Kathleen Mahoney, 207-217. Toronto: Carswell, 1987.

Tarnopolsky, Walter. "The Equality Rights in the Canadian Charter of Rights and Freedoms." *Canadian Bar Review* 61 (1983): 243-264.

Thornton, Margaret. "Feminist Jurisprudence: Illusion or Reality?" *Australian Journal of Law and Society* 3 (1986): 5-29.

Tress, Daryl McGowan. "Comment and Reply." *Signs* 14, 1 (Autumn 1988): 197-99.

Tronto, Joan. "Beyond Gender Difference To A Theory of Care." *Signs* 12, 4 (Summer 1987): 644-663.

Unger, Roberto Mangabeira. *Knowledge and Politics.* New York: The Free Press, 1975.

Vickers, Jill McCalla. "Major Equality Issues of the Eighties." In *Canadian Human Rights Yearbook 1983*, eds. Jean-Denis Archambeault and R. Paul Nadin-Davis, 47-72. Toronto: Carswell, 1983.

———. "Equality Theories and Their Results: Equality-Seeking in a Cold Climate." In *Righting the Balance,* eds. Lynn Smith *et al.,* 3-24. Toronto: Carswell, 1986.

Vizkelety, Béatrice. *Proving Discrimination in Canada.* Toronto: Carswell, 1987.

West, Robin. "Jurisprudence and Gender." *The University of Chicago Law Review* 55, 1 (Winter 1988): 1-72.

———. "Feminism, Critical Social Theory, And Law." Legal Workshop Series, Faculty of Law, University of Toronto, April 14, 1989.

Westen, Peter. "The Empty Idea Of Equality." *Harvard Law Review* 95, 3 (January 1982): 537-590.

Wikler, Norma J. "Identifiying and Correcting Judicial Gender Bias." In *Equality and Judicial Neutrality,* eds. Sheilah L. Martin and Kathleen Mahoney, 12-21. Toronto: Carswell, 1987.

Williams, Patricia J. "On Being The Object of Property." *Signs* 14, 1 (Autumn 1988): 5-24.

Williams, Robert A. Jr. "Taking Rights Aggressively: The Perils And Promise of Critical Legal Theory for Peoples of Color." *Law and Inequality* 5 (1987): 103-134.

Williams, Wendy. "American Equality Jurisprudence." In *Equality and Judicial Neutrality,* eds. Sheilah L. Martin and Kathleen Mahoney, 115-127. Toronto: Carswell, 1987.

————. "The Equality Crisis: Some Reflections on Culture, Courts, and Feminism." *Women's Rights Law Reporter* 7, 3 (Spring 1982): 175-200.

Wishnik, Heather Ruth. "To Question Everything: The Inquiries of Feminist Jurisprudence." *Berkeley Women's Law Journal* 64 (1986): 64-77.

Wolgast, Elizabeth. "Wrong Rights." *Hypatia* 2, 1 (Winter 1987): 25-43.

Worden, K.C. "Overshooting the Target: A Feminist Deconstruction of Legal Education." *The American University Law Review* 34 (1985): 1141-1156.

Zwarun, Suzanne. "Fetus's Rights Vs. Mother's Rights." *Chatelaine* (January 1988): 53, 92-94.

INDEX